Volume 2

Women Who Dared

52 more stories of Fearless Daredevils, Adventurers & Rebels

Words by Linda Skeers

Pictures by Livi Gosling

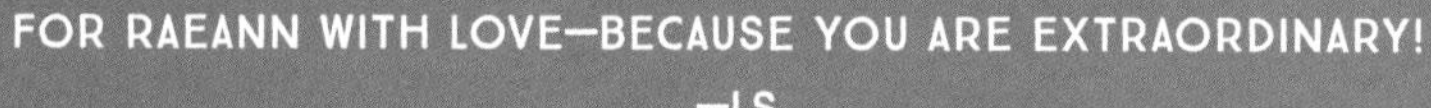

FOR RAEANN WITH LOVE—BECAUSE YOU ARE EXTRAORDINARY!
—LS

FOR MY DAUGHTER, WHO I HOPE WILL GROW UP TO BE JUST AS DARING AND WONDERFUL AS THESE AWESOME WOMEN.
—LG

The full color art was created by hand in ink and composed and colorized in Photoshop.

Published by Sourcebooks eXplore, an imprint of Sourcebooks Kids
P.O. Box 4410, Naperville, Illinois 60567-4410
(630) 961-3900
sourcebookskids.com

Cataloging-in-Publication Data is on file with the Library of Congress.

Source of Production: Toppan Leefung Printing Co., Ltd., Dongguan, Guangdong Province, China
Date of Production: February 2025
Run Number: 5044880

Printed and bound in China.
TL 10 9 8 7 6 5 4 3 2 1

CONTENTS

DAREDEVILS

ADVENTURERS

REBELS

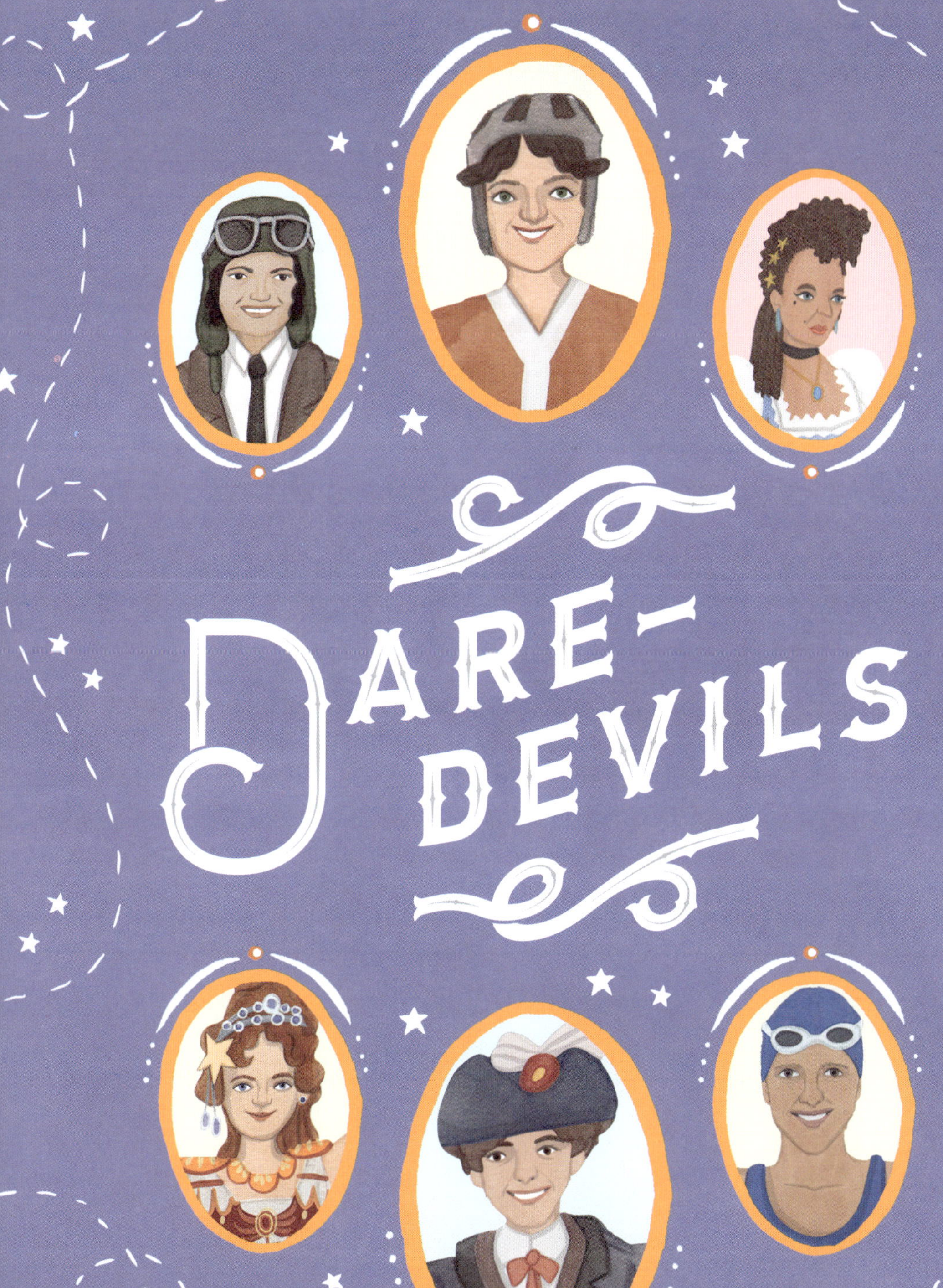

DARE-DEVILS

KATHERINE CHEUNG

* AWESOME AVIATOR *

Katherine grew up in China where her father was a businessman who frequently visited the United States. Her passion was music, so when she was seventeen years old, she moved to the U.S. to continue her studies at the Los Angeles Conservatory of Music and other schools.

Her father wanted her to learn how to drive, so he took her out by the airport where she could practice without having to deal with traffic. But Katherine had a hard time practicing because she was mesmerized by the airplanes taking off and landing. Now she had a new passion—flying!

She thought about returning to China to take lessons. But Chinese flying schools did not accept women. So, she studied music. Eventually she married and had two daughters. Her life was busy, yet she still dreamt of flying. It would take years before her dream became a reality.

Finally, when she was twenty-seven years old, she enrolled in aviation classes in Los Angeles at the Chinese Aeronautical Association. Her skill, aptitude, and passion were on full display—and after only 12 ½ hours of instruction, she was ready to take her first solo flight! She soon received her pilot's license—becoming the first Chinese American woman to do so.

Katherine loved flying, but she also liked to push the boundaries. She learned to do barrel rolls, loop the loops, spiral dives, and many other aerial acrobatics. She dazzled crowds at air shows all along the California coast with her daring and death-defying stunts.

Air races were popular at that time, and Katherine entered many along with other female pilots. One tough competitor was Amelia Earhart—who also became a good friend. Amelia invited Katherine to join an exclusive club for fellow female aviators called the Ninety-Nines. They encouraged other women to take flying lessons and take to the skies.

Katherine was always eager to learn something new, and in 1935, she earned her international commercial pilot's license. On one trip her plane's compass broke and she successfully navigated her way to the airport without it.

Katherine was recognized by the Smithsonian National Air and Space Museum as the nation's first Asian Aviatrix. In 2000, she was inducted into the Women in Aviation International's Pioneer Hall of Fame. Her courage and persistence have inspired other women to follow their passion and learn to fly.

LAURA DEKKER

* SENSATIONAL SAILOR *

It shouldn't be a surprise that Laura loved being on the water—she was born in New Zealand while her parents were sailing around the world. And their journey lasted another five years, so she spent her early years living on a boat!

For her sixth birthday, Laura received her own boat as a gift—an Optimist dinghy designed for children. She named it *Guppy* and learned how to sail it with her father on a Windsurfer nearby until she was ready to sail solo. Many more solo trips took place after that. She also read, studied navigation, and learned everything she could about sailing.

When she was twelve years old, it was time to really test her ability and knowledge as a sailor. With her dog Spot as her only companion, she went on a six-week sailing trip. It was a success! But Laura had a much bigger dream—to sail solo around the world.

To practice, she sailed between the Netherlands and England—facing strong winds and rough currents. It was scary, dangerous, exciting—and successful.

At fourteen, Laura was ready to set sail around the world! Except the Dutch government said NO! They felt she was too young to undertake such a trip. Laura disagreed and argued in court eight times for permission. And lost all eight times.

People around the world had strong opinions about her solo trip—some felt she should be allowed to sail alone; others felt it was much too dangerous for someone her age. Laura tried to ignore the hoopla surrounding her and just focused on doing what she loved most—sailing.

Finally, just before her fifteenth birthday, the government decided to let her parents decide if she could set sail.

They knew how skilled and responsible she was and agreed. With one condition—she had to keep up with her schoolwork while she was on her trip!

On August 21, 2010, Laura set sail from Gibraltar, across the Atlantic Ocean to the Caribbean island of St. Maarten. Some days were easy. Others were hard. When stressed, Laura played her flute.

During her journey she watched as dolphins and whales swam beside her boat. She ate a lot of cornflakes and canned beans. And had plenty of time to just enjoy the beauty around her and think.

On January 21, 2012, after a whopping 518 days and 27,000 miles, Laura landed back in St. Maarten. She'd achieved one dream—but is looking forward to even more adventures in the future!

1880–1964 FRANCE

MAURICIA DE TIERS

* DEATH-DEFYING DRIVER *

Mauricia was married, divorced, and working as a cashier in a bar by the age of twenty. Her life was ordinary and routine. Until she met a circus-loving artist!

He was always drawing plans for a new, bold act involving a car on a track and a huge steel loop. He knew it would be sensational—even among all the other wild performances popular in France at the time, but he hesitated to spend the time and money needed to build it. Because who would ever be brave enough to attempt the death-defying stunt?

Mauricia had never driven a car. Or rode a bicycle. But on an impulse, she volunteered! The car rode on a track, so how hard could it be? Besides, she doubted he would ever build such a contraption.

But he did.

And called it the "Dip of Death."

The steel scaffolding was taller than a three-story building. Before each performance, the car was raised by a strong cable and set on the track high above the crowd. Mauricia would climb into the driver's seat, release the lever, and zoom down the track as the audience held their breath.

The car would careen down, flip upside down, soar across a forty-five-foot gap, and (hopefully!) land right side up on the other side.

The incredible ride took a mere four seconds. But the memory of such a dazzling feat stayed with the crowd for a lifetime!

The act was a huge success, and in 1905, Mauricia was ready to perform before an American audience. The steel scaffolding, car, and equipment sailed to New York on a steamship. Once again, Mauricia astounded audiences with her extraordinary bravery and daring. She was paid $5,000 for each performance—often performing twice a day. She was earning more money every week than the U.S. president made in a year!

The act wasn't foolproof, and during one performance, the car left the track and crashed. Although injured, she survived. And it gave her time to think. She decided to stop courting death in the loop the loop and turned to safer pursuits—joining the circus as an acrobat! One of her signature moves was to do somersaults—on the back of a running horse!

After retiring from performing, Mauricia had one final act—as a mayor of a town in France—a position she held for over twenty years.

1876–1968 GERMANY

MARGARET GAST

* REBELLIOUS RACER *

Margaret was born in a small German village and immigrated to the United States as a teenager. She was hired as a nanny and while she taught the children German, they taught her English!

A popular pastime was bicycle riding. Leisurely pedaling along streets and trails, admiring the scenery. Too boring for Margaret! She joined the Century Road Club of America—a group of women whose goal was to ride one hundred miles as fast as they could.

They loved competing against each other and testing their endurance. No prizes, no publicity, just pure enjoyment. They started with two hundred-mile races and increased the distance to one thousand miles. They'd ride at breakneck speed back and forth along the road. The long, billowing skirts, which were the height of fashion, didn't suit them, so they wore bloomers instead.

And then the problems began. Many people thought it wasn't "ladylike" to race bicycles. And that women were too frail and delicate for such strenuous exercise. But no matter how many people complained, they weren't breaking any law, so they simply pedaled on.

In 1900, at age twenty-three, Margaret set a new world record by riding one thousand miles in ninety-nine hours and fifty-five minutes. But she wasn't satisfied. Her next endurance race was 2,000 miles long and lasted 222 hours where she barely stopped to eat or sleep. Because of her incredible speed and stamina, she was nicknamed the "Mile a Minute Girl."

Soon a newfangled invention caught her attention—the "motor bicycle." Margaret was instantly fascinated and soon began doing demonstrations for crowds at fairs and exhibitions. She took her motorcycle apart, and then put it back together. Most people had never seen a motorcycle before—or a female mechanic! Margaret would then dazzle the crowd with stunts, which led to her next adventure. She traveled the country performing her daredevil act The Wall of Death where she would ride in a huge wooden barrel. She had to maintain her speed or slip and tumble to the floor. Margaret continued her death-defying act for eight years until her frequent injuries convinced her to retire.

Margaret challenged the idea that women were frail, weak, and fearful and raced into the history books. She was inducted into the United States Bicycling Hall of Fame in 1993.

FLYING MERKEL
FLYING MERKEL

ELOISE "FOX" HASTINGS

COURAGEOUS COWGIRL

Eloise Fox was a free spirit and rebellious child. Her parents believed sending her to a convent school would tame her wild ways and turn her into a proper young lady.

It did NOT!

At sixteen years old, she ran away and joined a Wild West show where she excelled at roping, relay events, and sprints. She brought crowds to their feet when she stood on the back of a pony as it raced around the arena. That same year she married a fellow rodeo star, dropped "Eloise," and became known as Fox Hastings.

Fox was a hit at every performance. She stood out with her signature hat and flaming red hair adorned with huge bows while amazing fans with her strength and fearlessness.

At one event, her horse fell on top of her. Instead of quitting, she dusted herself off, got on another horse, and kept going—and the crowd loved it!

The most dangerous event in a rodeo was bulldogging. The rider would race their horse after a steer, launch themselves from their horse to the steer, grab it by its horns, and wrestle it to the ground. Only men competed.

Until Fox Hastings.

In 1924, Fox was the first woman to attempt bulldogging. And she wrestled a steer, which weighed ten times more than she did, to the ground in seconds. At the time, it was seen as a one-time exhibition. But for Fox, it was the start of a new career. Soon she was competing against men in bulldogging events across the country in front of thousands of rodeo fans.

Fox paid the price for her daring participation many times. She suffered concussions, broken bones, scrapes, and bruises. But as soon as her wounds healed, she was right back in the saddle, billed as the "only lady bulldogger."

Newspaper reporters weren't quite sure what to make of this fearless rodeo queen, who was also a wife. One account described her courage and bravery during events but also added that she was "a good cook and tidy housekeeper."

Bulldogging was eventually banned—not because of the risk to the riders, but because of the possible injury to the steers.

Fox continued her trick riding and roping, even performing for British royalty.

In 2011, Fox was honored by the National Cowgirl Museum and Hall of Fame for her courage and abilities in the rodeo ring.

1853-1932 ENGLAND

ADELAIDE HERRMANN

* MAGNIFICENT MAGICIAN *

While other girls her age were doing needlework or practicing their penmanship, Adelaide was studying acrobatics, dancing, and bicycle tricks. She craved a more exciting and adventurous life—and she found it when she married magician Alexander Herrmann and became his assistant.

Adelaide was sawed in half, levitated, shot from a cannon, and vanished before adoring audiences in theaters around the world. She often combined her love of illusion and dance to create new acts.

Both their extravagant show and marriage were huge successes—until Alexander unexpectedly died. Adelaide was heartbroken. And worried about the future of the entire cast and crew of their show. She made a bold announcement—the show would go on, and she would be the main attraction.

Up to that point in time, women were often assistants, but never magicians doing their own tricks. She certainly wasn't going to let that stop her!

Now Adelaide was the one to make others levitate and disappear! She saved the most dangerous and death-defying trick for the grand finale—the bullet catch.

Adelaide would hold a china plate in front of her as six soldiers marched onto the stage. They'd raise their weapons, aim, and fire!

The audience screamed, and some people ran for the exits. But when the smoke cleared, Adelaide held up the plate—which contained all six bullets.

The audience was shocked, amazed, and entertained—proving that a female magician *could* be the star of the show.

Nicknamed "The Queen of Magic," Adelaide continued performing for another thirty years, dazzling crowds with her favorite tricks—and creating new and more daring ones.

One popular trick involved Noah's ark being pulled onto the stage. It was opened to show the empty interior. As an assistant stood on the deck, poured water down a pipe into the empty space, and with a wave of a magic wand, Adelaide opened the ark once again and out strolled a long line of animals—two by two—including dogs, ducks, zebras, and lions (or, if you looked closely, dogs dressed as lions).

Adelaide encouraged other women to study magic and wrote articles for the *Woman's Home Companion* magazine where she revealed the secret behind some of her tricks.

Adelaide's career was long and successful due to her hard work, talent, charisma—and maybe a little bit of magic.

GLADYS INGLE

* AERIAL ACROBAT *

From the time she was a young girl, Gladys was always looking for ways to combine her incredible sense of balance and love of heights. She'd skip atop fences, the higher the better! Once she built a pair of wooden stilts so tall she could only get on them from the roof of the house. Soon, she was parachuting out of hot-air balloons.

In the 1920s, many young women were drawn to Hollywood and aspired to be a star on the big screen. Gladys was no exception, but she found a unique and daring way to pursue her dream!

Gladys was fascinated by flying and was the fourth licensed female pilot in the United States. Not content to be in the pilot's seat, she was more comfortable outside the plane, standing on the wing. No parachute. No safety devices. No problem.

She became a popular aerial daredevil who performed amazing stunts in the movies. But Gladys wanted a new thrill, and in 1924, she found it. A group of former World War I pilots had created an aerial stunt team called the 13 Black Cats. Gladys became the first female member. They performed in movies and newsreels with a camera mounted on the plane to give audiences a bird's-eye view of their fearless feats.

They also performed at air shows and Gladys was always searching for another death-defying trick to dazzle the crowds. She would hang by her knees or stand on her head as the plane flew over 70 miles an hour or she'd walk back and forth—blindfolded—or shoot arrows at a target.

Her signature stunt was to jump from one plane to another—which she successfully accomplished over three hundred times!

The 13 Black Cats saved the most impressive stunt for their grand finale. As a plane circled above the crowd, a wheel would fall off the landing gear. The announcer would tell the frightened fans the plane was bound to crash. But Gladys would take off with a pilot in another plane, jump to the first plane with a tool kit and spare tire strapped to her back, and proceed to put on the new wheel to the roar of an adoring and relieved crowd.

Gladys is remembered as one of the bravest, most daring aerial acrobats to ever grace the skies.

MARIE MARVINGT

OUTSTANDING OVERACHIEVER

As a young girl, Marie never met a sport she didn't like—or excel at! Her father encouraged her as she mastered everything from bobsledding to boxing and ice-skating to swimming. She loved competing and frequently won championships in dozens of different sports.

Marie loved reading about explorers and adventurers and wanted to try *everything*—no matter how difficult or dangerous.

When she was only fifteen years old she paddled a canoe almost 250 miles. She also loved mountain-climbing and scaled almost every peak in the Alps. Not even barely surviving an avalanche put a damper on her enthusiasm!

Hot-air ballooning also became a passion, and she was the first female balloon pilot to fly from Paris to Europe, crossing the North Sea and the English Channel in treacherous weather conditions.

A year after she took her first airplane ride, she earned her pilot's license. Flying became a lifelong love and she made over nine hundred successful flights.

In between competitions and new endeavors, Marie studied medicine, astronomy, painting, singing, sculpting, and learned to speak four languages.

In 1907, Marie won first place in an international shooting competition against army military marksmen. Marie was a bicycling enthusiast and entered the Tour de France in 1908 but was refused entry because she was a woman. So, she simply rode behind the men and came in thirty-sixth. People took notice of her incredible athleticism, and in 1910, the French Academy of Sports awarded her a gold medal for all sports, the only one ever awarded! Marie earned the nickname "the Fiancée of Danger" for her daring endeavors.

As Marie got older, she decided to turn her love of aviation into a way of helping others. She wanted to create an aerial ambulance service where pilots and nurses could fly into a battle zone, pick up the wounded, and fly them to safety. To inform others of her idea, she attended over three thousand conferences around the world. Marie also designed a training course for nurses and became the first certified flight nurse herself. She created the Flying Ambulance Corps and recruited other women to serve as pilots and medical personnel.

But her adventuring days weren't over yet! At eighty, she received her helicopter license, and at eighty-six, she biked 175 miles across the French countryside—in the winter.

It's no wonder Marie is known as one of France's greatest heroines!

MUSTANG
ROLLER DERBY

PATTI MCGEE

SENSATIONAL SKATEBOARDER

Growing up in San Diego gave Patti lots of opportunities to be outside and active. And she took full advantage of that! She got her first bike when she was four years old. Then came roller skates. And a scooter.

Being adventurous came naturally to Patti—so did competing. She won a yo-yo championship and a kite-flying championship. She was also a swimmer and a high-diver. But surfing was her passion, and she won many awards for her skill and technique on the waves.

When Patti was a teenager, her brother did something that completely changed her life. He stole the wheels off her roller skates! Then he attached them to a smooth wooden board—and just like that, he had a homemade skateboard.

Patti certainly wasn't going to let him have all the fun—after all, they were *her* wheels! They skated in parking lots, on streets—anywhere there was a bit of concrete. Zipping down a steep hill felt like surfing a huge wave, and Patti loved it!

Next came the tricks and stunts. And more practicing. In 1964, Santa Monica held the First National Skateboard Contest. Of course, Patti entered. She completed the obstacle course, deftly skating around cones. And then did a perfect figure eight. For the freestyle event, she did something nobody had ever done before in a competition. She did a rolling handstand on her skateboard. The crowd was impressed—and so were the judges. Patti won!

The skateboard craze was spreading across the country—and Patti was right in the middle of it. At nineteen, she was featured on the cover of *Life* magazine doing her signature handstand, which got her national attention. Next came appearances on talk shows. She was even a guest on the television show *What's My Line?* where a panel had to guess what she did for a living.

Soon Patti was traveling across the country demonstrating Hobie skateboards and representing the company. Patti was now the first professional female skateboarder!

In 2010, she accomplished another milestone by being the first woman inducted into the Skateboarding Hall of Fame. And now that skateboarding is an Olympic event, she's inspiring even more girls to participate in the sport she loved.

DIANA NYAD

SENSATIONAL SWIMMER

Diana LOVED being in the water! By junior high, she was taking her swimming lessons and training seriously. She practiced for hours before school and again after school. She won three Florida high school championships—but that was only the beginning of her long career.

She pushed herself to train harder and for longer distances—soon she was excelling as a marathon swimmer. Pool closed? No problem! Diana enjoyed swimming in any available body of water—lakes, rivers, even oceans!

With a bit of a rebellious streak, Diana liked to push the boundaries and do what others didn't think was possible. When she was twenty-five years old, she decided to swim around the island of Manhattan. The water was filthy, smelly, and so contaminated she became sick and couldn't finish. Refusing to give up, she tried again. After eight long hours, she succeeded! Both the *New York Times* and former First Lady Jackie Kennedy were impressed by her accomplishment.

Diana was always setting new goals and big dreams for herself. The biggest was to be the first person to swim from Havana, Cuba, to Key West, Florida. The 110-mile trip would be extremely treacherous. Many had tried. All had failed.

Was it even possible?

Diana was determined to find out. But it certainly wouldn't happen right away. Thankfully, she had an abundance of patience.

During the next *thirty-five years*, she made four fateful attempts.

She failed four times.

She encountered storms, high winds, exhaustion, and bone-numbing temperatures. And then there were the incredibly painful stings from the venomous box jellyfish, which ended her attempts—and almost her life.

If those weren't enough hardships to overcome, she was swimming through shark-infested waters—without the aid of a shark cage. Instead, she relied on her shark spotters on a support boat, which lessened the danger, but didn't get rid of it.

Although she worked as a sportscaster for thirty of those years, Diana never gave up on her dream. In 2013, when she was sixty-four years old, she made her fifth attempt. She wore a specially designed suit to protect her from the jellyfish—even her lips were covered. It was heavy and cumbersome but necessary.

On August 31, Diana stepped into the ocean in Cuba. Fifty-two long, exhausting hours later, she stepped onto the shore in Florida!

Diana had done it! She is a living tribute to the word "persistence"!

FLORIDA
Key West
Havana
CUBA

Kitty O'Neil

KITTY O'NEIL

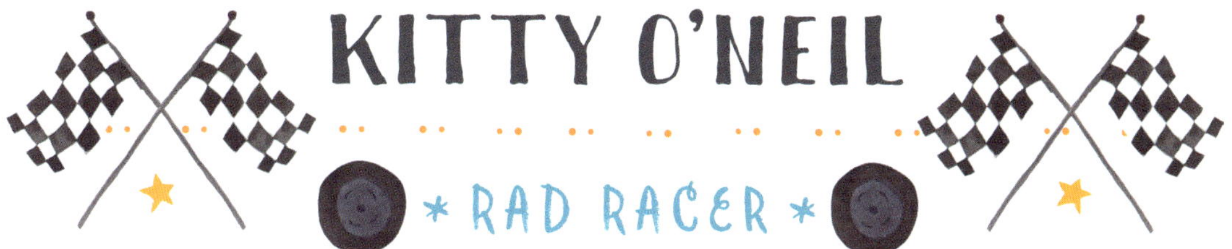

* RAD RACER *

Kitty was only five months old when she was struck by a trio of diseases—measles, mumps, and chicken pox. She recovered but lost her hearing.

She learned to read lips and sound out words by holding her hand to her mother's throat when she spoke.

Being deaf didn't slow her down when it came to being active—in fact, she wanted to try everything and do it fast!

She loved swimming and decided to join the diving team. But the coach would shout directions she couldn't hear when the divers were practicing—twist right, twist left, flip. The solution? He'd fire a gun loaded with blanks when she was to change directions. She didn't hear the gun, but she felt the vibration. Before long, Kitty was a champion diver!

Illness struck again—this time, meningitis. Kitty's recovery was long and brutal, but when she did recover, she wanted to try even more exciting and thrilling activities like scuba diving, hang gliding, and skydiving.

But most of all, Kitty loved speed—the faster the better! And it didn't matter if it was on land or on the water. In 1970, she broke a water-skiing record by going 104.85 miles per hour. She also raced speedboats, motorcycles, race cars, and snowmobiles.

Soon her love of extreme sports and the thrill of danger landed her a job as a stuntwoman. Her high-fall of 127 feet off a twelve-story building into an airbag was a record breaker. Until she fell 180 feet from a helicopter, breaking her own record!

She was much sought-after to perform daredevil stunts and car chases for television shows and movies. Kitty was always up for a challenge, and in 1976, a new opportunity presented itself, and she couldn't turn it down.

Kitty was going to attempt a land speed record by driving the SMI Motivator—a rocket-powered car! Not only was there a problem of the car going airborne and crashing, but Kitty could black out and lose control.

She knew the risks but didn't hesitate to get behind the wheel. Kitty set a new land speed record of 618 miles per hour! That meant she covered a mile in a mere fifteen seconds! It took three parachutes and five miles to finally stop the rocket car.

Kitty's fast and fearless record-breaking successes earned her the nickname the "fastest woman on earth." She never let her gender or deafness slow her down—and she courageously led the way for future racers.

KATHARINA PAULUS

PIONEERING PARACHUTIST

As a child, Katharina often used the family's clothesline as a tightrope, practicing acrobatics with grace and daring.

When she was nineteen years old, her father died and she worked as a seamstress, like her mother, to help support the family. A few years later she was hired by Hermann Lattemann for her skills, but not to sew clothes—to repair hot-air balloons!

The two eventually married and Katharina decided to do more than just repair balloons. In 1893, she joined her husband in his aerial show and became the first German woman to attempt a parachute jump (and only the third in the world)! Hot-air ballooning and aerial acrobatics was a popular—and dangerous—form of entertainment. And Katharina loved it.

Parachutes at that time were rudimentary, cumbersome, and large. They were difficult to handle, and there was always the danger of the ropes getting tangled during the descent. But the duo continued performing for thousands of enthusiastic fans. Until tragedy struck.

In 1895, as the two jumped from the balloon, Katharina's chute opened. Hermann's did not, and he died instantly.

Katharina went into mourning for months—wondering if there was anything she could have done to help avoid the accident. She never wanted that to happen to another parachutist.

Fans and supporters wrote her thousands of letters encouraging her to perform again. She agreed and started touring again under the stage name "Miss Polly." When she wasn't dazzling audiences with her daring acrobatics, she was busy inventing a safer parachute. One that could be carefully folded and worn like a backpack that had its ropes fastened into the cloth to avoid tangling.

In 1915, Katharina applied for a patent for a collapsible parachute she called a "rescue apparatus for aeronauts." The patent was granted and her invention became a lifesaver!

She remained a star attraction at aerial shows, adding an even more amazing feat. Wearing a sailor suit, black boots, and a jaunty white cap, she would jump out of a hot-air balloon, open a chute, take it off, and while the crowd gasped, would open another parachute and glide to the ground.

She was making parachutes in her apartment when the German government placed an order for seven thousand. Seamstresses were hired to help, but she cut each one by hand.

News of her invention spread, and she was awarded patents in Austria and Switzerland—and soon other countries were interested in her design and worked on improvements.

Katharina's courage and creativity have helped generations of parachuting adventurers, soldiers, and pilots land safely.

Fig1
Fig2
Fig3

ROSSA RICHTER

* COURAGEOUS CANNONBALL *

Rossa's parents both worked for the circus, which made her childhood rather unconventional. While other kids were learning the alphabet, she was learning acrobatics. While they learned their times tables, she learned tightrope walking. By age six, she was performing before huge crowds.

As a child she also took ballet lessons and did gymnastics. Both activities helped increase her strength, balance, and agility. Rossa was becoming a strong and talented athlete.

When she was just a teenager, she began performing her most daring and dangerous stunt. Wearing a scarlet leotard and pink tights (scandalous at that time!), she would scoot inside a huge cannon. The fuse would be lit with a dramatic flair. Gasps from the audience were heard as smoke swirled into the air. Then, a bone-shaking *BOOM*! Rossa would be shot out of the cannon, soar through the air, and land in a safety net—much to the delight and relief of the crowd.

Rossa still did aerial tricks on the trapeze and showcased her amazing balancing abilities on the tightrope, but the human cannonball act drew in audiences all over Europe and the United States.

It also drew criticism. Many people didn't believe such a dangerous stunt should be considered "entertainment." Especially when performed by a young woman. Lawmakers got involved and wanted to prohibit such acts. Rossa defended her performance and called it "art." While both sides debated the issue, Rossa continued to dazzle audiences as a human cannonball.

Safety nets were such an important part of her act that Rossa realized they could have practical uses outside of the circus. She began educating fire departments on how nets could help save people trapped in burning buildings. To get her message across, she jumped out of the window of a tall building—and landed safely in a net. The New York Fire Department thanked her for her contribution to public safety.

Was Rossa *really* a "human cannonball"?

Yes. And no.

The "cannon" was a painted metal tube, not a military weapon. Gunpowder and firecrackers added to the noise and drama, but Rossa was actually catapulted out by a spring-loaded platform. Even though it was a trick—it still took courage to perform and paved the way for future generations of daring stunts, acts, and performances by fearless women.

KATIE SANDWINA

* SENSATIONAL STRONGWOMAN *

With both parents and her thirteen siblings being circus performers, it was a given that Katie Brumbach would follow in their footsteps. As a toddler, she did handstands balancing on her father's arm. By the time she was sixteen years old, she was over six feet tall and incredibly strong, and that became her claim to fame.

Her father would offer prize money to any man who could beat her in a wrestling match. Many tried. They all failed!

But Max Heymann wasn't bothered by losing to a teenager—instead, he ended up marrying her and joining their circus family. He even let Katie lift him up over her head with one hand during performances.

Katie wasn't the only one doing feats of strength at that time. Eugene Sandow was hailed as the strongest man in the world. And he just happened to be in a New York audience when Katie challenged anyone to come forward and lift more weight than she could.

He confidently marched onto the stage. They lifted weights, added more, and kept lifting. Katie managed to lift three hundred pounds over her head. It was Sandow's turn. He could only raise the weight to his chest. Katie had defeated him!

Her victory made newspaper headlines across the country, and she changed her last name from Brumbach to Sandwina to help cement her title as the "world's strongest woman."

Katie kept adding more astonishing feats of strength to her act that included juggling cannonballs, lifting live horses, bending iron bars, and breaking iron chains with her bare hands.

Her performance became even more elaborate when she balanced a carousel on her shoulders that held fourteen riders! It seemed her strength knew no bounds. She even performed her balancing act hours after she gave birth to her son.

Katie's popularity and fame also gave her a platform to advocate for causes near and dear to her heart. She was especially interested in women's rights and while working for the Barnum & Bailey Circus, she became the vice president of a suffrage group. She was frequently written about in newspapers and earned the nickname "Sandwina the Suffragette."

Katie continued to perform onstage and amaze audiences until her sixties. Then she and her husband Max opened a restaurant. But every now and then, Katie would surprise customers by bending iron bars, straightening horseshoes, or lifting Max high over her head while customers dined.

MARIA SPELTERINI

* TERRIFIC TIGHTROPE WALKER *

Maria was born in Livorno, Italy, to a circus family. So, it was no surprise that she started performing daredevil stunts when she was only three years old!

As she got older, she specialized in walking the tightrope—especially over raging rivers with just a long pole to help her balance. She performed to awestruck crowds in several countries in Europe. In 1876, she decided to reach a larger audience and took her act to New York.

For a twenty-five-cent ticket, you could watch her do stunts on a two-inch high wire like walking backwards, skipping, and balancing on a chair ON the wire—all while wearing a dazzling costume.

Maria tried to get permission from the city to walk a tightrope across the Brooklyn Bridge, which was still being constructed. Her request was denied because it was deemed far too dangerous.

She set her sights on another location—Niagara Falls! It was the United States' Centennial and celebrations were being held around the country—and Maria decided to be a part of it. The day after her twenty-third birthday, she donned a scarlet tunic with a sparkling green vest and green boots and became the first woman to cross Niagara Falls on a tightrope. Before a cheering crowd of over two thousand spectators, while two bands played, she walked over and back. She gracefully and calmly ignored the gusting wind, the cold, stinging spray, and the thunderous noise from the Falls. It appeared almost effortless, so to add drama, she strapped her feet into wicker peach baskets and did it again.

But she was just getting started!

Next, she wore a blindfold and placed a paper bag over her head to make sure she couldn't see anything—and walked across again. And skipped back! The crowds held their breath during those death-defying ten minutes. For her grand finale, she placed handcuffs on her wrists and ankles and crossed once more.

The crowds loved her! And so did the press. Articles and photographs of the daring funambulist (a fancy name for tightrope walker) showed up in newspapers across the country. She was nicknamed "The Heroine of Niagara."

Maria continued to perform her dazzling high-wire act across Europe, drawing in huge crowds of adoring fans. She will be long remembered as the first, and so far, only woman to ever attempt to walk across the gorge at Niagara Falls.

ELISABETH THIBLE

BRAVE BALLOONIST

Details about Elisabeth's childhood are scarce—except that she became a popular opera singer as a young woman. But she proved to have a brave and daring side to her too!

The very first hot-air balloons took to the skies in early 1784 and soon balloon mania swept across France. Only six months later, the popular diva was asked to climb aboard an ornate blue-and-yellow balloon named *La Gustave*, named after King Gustav III of Sweden. He was in France to watch this spectacular event.

But she wasn't the first choice to share the basket with Monsieur Fleurant—a painter and enthusiastic aeronaut. That honor was bestowed upon King Gustav himself, but he was too scared of this newfangled flying contraption and refused!

Being a bit of a celebrity, Elisabeth wasn't going to take flight in ordinary clothes. Instead, she dressed as Minerva, the Roman goddess of wisdom, art, and war, in a lace-covered gown and large feathered hat. The thousands of spectators were shocked to see a *woman* do something so outrageous and incredibly dangerous!

She wasn't the first woman to take a balloon ride, but she was the first to take one that was untethered—no safety ropes would tie the balloon to the ground.

The crowd watched in awe as Elisabeth and Monsieur Fleurant ascended into the sky waving a flag as drums played. But the spectacle didn't end there. The two serenaded the crowds with opera duets. Besides singing, Elisabeth also helped stoke the chafing-dish firebox that kept the balloon aloft during the entire forty-five-minute trip. They reached an altitude of 8,500 feet and soared about three miles. It was the longest and highest successful balloon flight at that time in history.

The flight itself was uneventful, but the landing was rough. Just as they hit the ground, the silk balloon burst open and fell on top of them. Monsieur Fleurant took out a knife and cut himself out of the silk. Elisabeth managed to untangle herself but sprained an ankle in the process.

Frantic bystanders rushed to their aid, which caused the balloon to fall onto the firebox and go up in flames. While *La Gustave* burned, Elisabeth was carried in triumph to meet King Gustav III himself, who was thrilled with the demonstration.

And Elisabeth soared into the history books as a brave and daring aeronaut!

ADVEN-
TURERS

1799-1871 ENGLAND

ANNA ATKINS

GROUNDBREAKING BOTANIST

In the early 1800s, educating girls wasn't much of a priority. But Anna's mother died when she was a baby, so she was raised by her father. And he was a well-respected scientist who shared his knowledge with his curious daughter.

Anna's childhood was one long, continuous science lesson, and the English fields, meadows, and seashores were her classroom.

She helped her father catch and study insects in their home laboratory. Thousands of insects!

Anna also collected leaves, flowers, and plants. To preserve them, she placed the specimen between the pages of a heavy book until it dried out. Then she'd carefully mount and label it.

One of her favorite pastimes was going to the beach where she gathered shells, plants, driftwood, and seaweed—she *loved* seaweed!

Anna was also an incredible artist who created intricate and detailed drawings of her finds. Her sketches were so remarkable that her father used over 250 of them to illustrate his book *Lamarck's Genera of Shells*.

Her father was a member of the Royal Society of London, where scientists gathered to discuss their findings. Anna had so much knowledge to share, after studying plants for years, but she wasn't able. Women were NOT allowed.

Anna refused to let that damper her enthusiasm to learn even more about the natural world. She continued to collect and dry plants. If only there was a way to capture an image permanently! Cameras were in the early stages of development and not very reliable. But Anna wouldn't let that stop her either—she'd take photos *without* a camera!

She created cyanotypes by placing a specimen on paper coated with chemicals and then setting it in direct sunlight. Later, after removing the specimen, she was left with an intricate white print on a blue background. The image was permanent and could be reproduced and shared with others.

And that's how Anna created the first book of photographic images showcasing her extensive collection of seaweed. *British Algae: Cyanotype Impressions* eventually had two additional volumes and was studied and admired by scientists and botanists worldwide. She was finally getting the recognition and respect she deserved.

During her career, Anna created over ten thousand prints by hand. The beautiful white-on-blue images combined science and art and can be seen and admired in many museums today.

DOROTHEA BATE

PIONEERING PALEONTOLOGIST

Growing up in England, Dorothea spent her childhood exploring the countryside and nearby coast. She collected shells, plants, bones, beetles, feathers, and fossils. She spent very little time in school but learned everything she could about the natural world around her.

When she was nineteen years old, her passion led her to the Natural History Museum in London. Despite the facts they had never hired a woman and she lacked any formal training, she convinced them to hire her—and they did!

She was tasked with sorting species in the Bird Room. Her years of bird-watching and collecting feathers helped her excel at her job, but she longed to get back out into nature. At twenty-two, she was one of the first paleontologists to explore the limestone caves of Cyprus.

Dorothea continued collecting insects, mice, small mammals, birds, and bones—and sent over two hundred specimens back to the museum to exhibit. When her funding ran out, she paid for her expedition out of her own pocket.

Finding new areas to explore meant scrambling down cliffs, blazing a trail through the bush, and crawling into caves. She would painstakingly chip away at the rock walls searching for fossils. Even when she contracted malaria and had a high fever, she continued chipping away. Days turned into weeks; weeks turned into months.

Her persistence was rewarded when she discovered bones and teeth. But *what* exactly had she uncovered? It didn't look like anything ever seen before! After much research and studying, Dorothea concluded it was a species of extinct pygmy elephants—which had never been known to live on Cyprus! She had the honor of naming this new species—*Elephas cypriotes.*

She also discovered a bizarre new species that had rodent-like teeth but the body of a goat-like antelope. She called it *Myotragus*, which means "mouse goat."

Scientists today are still studying and learning new information from her fossilized finds. Her dwarf Cretan elephant has been deemed to be the world's smallest mammoth—no bigger than a dog!

From talking herself into a job to her amazing contributions to paleontology, ornithology, and zoology, Dorothea spent her life learning about the natural world and sharing her knowledge with generations of curious researchers and future scientists.

ANNE INNIS DAGG

* JOYOUS GIRAFFOLOGIST *

Anne was four years old when she saw her first giraffe at the zoo. It was love at first sight! She was fascinated by the tall, majestic animals and wanted to know everything about them. Unfortunately, nobody had done extensive research on them, so information was scarce.

Her father was a professor and her mother a writer, so she grew up in a family that loved to learn. She obtained a degree in biology and a masters in genetics. But what she really wanted to study was giraffes.

Anne wrote to several universities for funding. They all turned her down—because she was a woman, and they didn't believe she could handle the rigors of on-site research. Refusing to give up, she wrote another letter to a ranch in South Africa in 1956. This time she signed it *A. Innis*. She was invited to come and paid her own way there.

Anne was the first dedicated scientist to observe and take meticulous notes about giraffes in the wild. She watched them from sunrise to sunset, documenting everything they did. She realized each one had unique markings and soon was able to tell them apart—and give them names. She collected leaves from the trees they nibbled on to understand their eating habits and diet.

She shared her knowledge through books and articles. Even though she was considered to be the first giraffologist, she was repeatedly denied tenure as a professor—by all-male committees. Disheartened, she refused to give up and continued to add to her body of knowledge about her beloved giraffes.

Anne was now advocating for giraffes and for women to succeed in academia. Both were struggles she was determined to win!

By 1972, she was calling herself a "citizen scientist," which fit her perfectly. A few years later, her book *The Giraffe: Its Biology, Behavior, and Ecology* became the foremost authority among animal researchers, scientists, and zoologists around the world.

She continued to speak out about the plight of giraffes and the importance of preserving their habitat. And the importance of women to follow their dreams no matter the obstacles.

In 2018, the documentary *The Woman Who Loves Giraffes* helped get her the recognition she so richly deserves. And three of those universities that turned her down for tenure? They apologized!

Anne continued to receive awards and honors, but her focus had always been, and always would be, on protecting her beloved giraffes.

The Indian Ocean
Alice Springs

ROBYN DAVIDSON

NOTEWORTHY NOMAD

Robyn loved exploring outdoors as a child. As a young woman she dreamt of just leaving all her belongings behind and setting out into the unknown. That sense of wanderlust grew stronger through the years.

She had a series of odd jobs, moved frequently, and searched for meaning in her life. Then she got an idea—a big, bold, wild idea! She would hike across her beloved Australian outback and really dig deep into who she was as a person. It would be a journey of self-exploration.

This would be a trip that would take years of planning and preparation. She would need to travel with camels to help carry her supplies. Did she know much about camels?

Nope!

But she was willing to learn. With only six dollars, a small suitcase with a few clothes, and big expectations, she started out in Alice Springs, Australia. She spent almost two years learning about camels, taking care of them, and training them. They weren't easy animals to work with, but they were essential to her success.

She soon learned that camels could be prone to injuries and infections, and veterinarian bills were expensive. She worried that her trip was doomed before it even got started. How would she ever earn enough money to cover her bills?

Robyn was at a crossroads. The trip was meant to be private and personal. But when *National Geographic* magazine heard of her endeavor, they offered her $4,000 to write about her experience. She was conflicted but finally agreed.

In 1977, at twenty-seven years old, she started out accompanied by four camels and her dog, Diggity.

Robyn walked twenty to thirty miles a day under a blazing sun. She encountered scorpions, huge millipedes, and many, many snakes!

She had maps but preferred navigating by the stars. At times, hiking was easy. Other times, she had to crawl up sand dunes, slide down the other side, and then do it again—day after day.

Robyn walked for weeks without seeing another human being and then would come across a band of nomads. She earned the nickname "camel lady" and news of her trip spread among the Aboriginal people, who were delighted to meet her.

Nine months later, she arrived at her destination—the Indian Ocean. She learned that the journey itself wasn't hard but braving to take the first step toward the unknown can be—but it's worth it.

THURIDUR EINARSDOTTIR

UNCONVENTIONAL SEA CAPTAIN

Iceland wasn't the easiest place to raise a family. The weather was rough, fishing was dangerous, and food was scarce.

Then life got even harder! In 1783, a series of earthquakes shook the land. Next, a lava-spewing volcano erupted. Ash covered everything—and poisoned fish, killed livestock, and ruined crops. Thousands died; others moved away. But Thuridur's family stayed and survived the yearlong famine by eating seaweed.

Eventually, fishing began again. And this time, eleven-year-old Thuridur wanted to accompany her father. It meant braving rough seas, frigid temperatures, and icy winds for twelve hours without a break.

Still, Thuridur was ready. But women at that time were forbidden to wear trousers, only long, heavy, and cumbersome woolen skirts. If she fell overboard, she'd immediately sink. So, Thuridur did the unthinkable. She donned her brother's leather pants and climbed into the rowboat!

The crew was skeptical—until she snagged the first fish! She wore her brother's gloves to protect her hands from the elements, but they were too big. She tossed them off, grabbed the line with her bare hands, and hauled in her catch. And then caught another and another and another.

She had proved herself and became a regular member of the crew. Besides being a talented and successful fisherwoman, she excelled at reading the skies and predicting the weather—which made her an even more valuable crew member.

When Thuridur was fourteen, her father died, and she began fishing on other boats. She watched as one captain berated his crew and shouted orders. To avoid mutiny, she spoke up on behalf of the crew and became known for her skills at conflict resolution.

On another trip, the open-air rowboat was caught in a storm. Two men were swept overboard! The captain said it was too dangerous to rescue them.

Thuridur told him his job was to be responsible for the boat and its crew, expecting him to back down and attempt a rescue.

He didn't.

So, she stepped in and gave the crew orders—and the men were saved.

She had earned the crew's loyalty and respect and vowed not to work under another captain again. Secretly recruiting her own crew, she became captain of her own boat.

Thuridur fished the turbulent Icelandic seas for over fifty-two years and never lost a crew member. At sixty-three, she retired as captain—but remained working on boats as a deckhand!

ICELAND
ICELAND

BIRUTÉ GALDIKAS

* PASSIONATE PRIMATOLOGIST *

Biruté was born in Lithuania but grew up in Canada. One of her favorite books as a child was *Curious George*, a story about a mischievous monkey. Biruté was fascinated and was soon reading stacks of books about primates. At a very early age she knew she wanted to spend her life learning about these amazing creatures.

During graduate school she was close to making her dream come true—but her professors told her studying orangutans in the wild was impossible. They were too elusive, their habitat too remote, and it was just too dangerous.

Biruté disagreed. She boldly spoke to the famous anthropologist Dr. Louis Leakey after hearing his lecture and told him of her plan. Since very little was known about orangutans, Leakey agreed to help by persuading the National Geographic Society to fund a research facility in a remote spot in Borneo's rainforest. Still, many doubted that she would ever even *see* one of the elusive orangutans. But she was undeterred.

There were no roads leading to their tiny outpost. No phones, no mail, no comforts of home. There were plenty of poisonous snakes, animals, and insects. Searching for orangutans was dangerous and uncomfortable—and Biruté loved every second of it.

And finally—there they were! Success at last! Biruté carefully watched the orangutans and took copious notes of everything they did. Slowly, she earned their trust and after four years of meticulous observations, she published her amazing research. Biruté was the first person to discover orangutans are fruit eaters and she compiled a list of over four hundred different foods they consume!

For the first time, orangutans were getting the respect and admiration they deserved. They are incredibly intelligent and can learn sign language, make and use tools to help gather food, and are extremely nurturing—mother orangutans spend years caring for and teaching their offspring—all activities Biruté saw up close and personal.

The more Biruté learned about orangutans, the more worried she became about their dwindling habitat. Humans were destroying rainforests by harvesting trees at an incredible rate. The orangutan's homeland was shrinking—how would they survive and thrive without human intervention? She created Orangutan Foundation International and raised millions of dollars to preserve rainforests and create sanctuaries and rehabilitation facilities for injured orangutans. In 1977, she received Indonesia's highest honor—the Hero of the Earth Award—the first woman to do so.

Biruté has spent nearly fifty years studying orangutans in the wild and has amassed an extraordinary amount of data on them. She works tirelessly to raise awareness of the importance of preserving rainforests and habitats—and she's making a difference.

1954- PERU

JULIANE KOEPCKE

New high school graduate Juliane was taking a Christmas Eve flight in 1971 with her mother. They were soaring over Peru on their way to the research facility in the Amazon rainforest where both her parents worked.

Suddenly, the plane was struck by lightning and plummeted two miles to the ground. Miraculously, Juliane survived the crash—still strapped into her seat. But she had a severe gash in her arm, a broken collarbone, and a concussion. And her glasses were missing.

Juliane knew that a quick rescue was unlikely. The rainforest was too thick for her to be spotted by planes. And it could take days, maybe weeks, before a search party found her. It was up to her to save herself. Without food. Without water. And no idea which way to go.

Juliane remembered something her father had taught her—to follow the water. Hopefully it would lead to civilization. It was her only option, so she stood still and listened. When she heard the faint burbling of a tiny stream, she started hiking. Through the dense jungle. Over rocks and logs. Constantly swatting biting insects and watching out for snakes and spiders. Her skin burned and blistered. She grew weaker every hour.

When the stream became a river, she decided to float rather than continue hiking. She worried about piranhas, crocodiles, stingrays, and snakes. Yet, she kept going. Over a week after the crash, she spotted a small boat. Was it real or a hallucination?

It was real! And nearby was an empty shack. She crawled inside to rest.

And that's where three men found her—alive.

They took Juliane by canoe to a village where she was given medical care. Then she was flown to a missionary post. Soon, she was reunited with her father.

Sadly, she was the only survivor of the crash.

Against all odds, Juliane survived by sheer will and determination. And she dedicated her life to help the Amazon rainforest survive—and thrive—by creating a nature reserve on the site of her parents research facility.

INK
TABLETS
FOR
MILITARY USE

DOROTHY LAWRENCE

* FEARLESS FREELANCER *

Little is known about Dorothy's earliest years except that she was adopted by a guardian of the Church of England.

She did receive an education and excelled at writing. She hoped to become a successful journalist and sold articles on a variety of topics to newspapers and magazines as a freelance writer.

When WWI began, Dorothy had a new goal—to become a war correspondent and report from the front lines. But not a single newspaper would hire a woman—and many even turned away male journalists because the job would be far too dangerous for civilians.

Dorothy refused to give up. At age eighteen, she rode a bicycle through the French countryside to Paris. She befriended two British soldiers in a café and persuaded them to smuggle out a uniform for her. They agreed to help because they believed she would never get close to the front lines.

But they hadn't counted on her drive and ambition. She transformed herself from a teenage girl to a respectable-looking soldier by padding the shoulders of the uniform, cutting her hair short, and forging military identity papers with her "new" name, Private Denis Smith.

She met a trench-digging soldier who saw through her disguise. Being unable to talk her out of her mission, he decided to help. Dorothy spent her nights in an abandoned cottage in the forest, eating any rations he and his fellow soldiers could spare from their own meals.

For ten long days, Dorothy worked alongside men in the trenches. Between the grueling work, stress, and unhealthy conditions, she soon became ill. To protect the men who had aided her and to seek medical assistance, she turned herself in to the unit's commander.

That wasn't the end of her ordeal. She was promptly placed under military arrest and later interrogated as a spy. Why else would a woman infiltrate a troop on the front lines?

Having breached what should have been a secure and impenetrable camp, she was an embarrassment to the army. A judge ordered her to remain in France and sign a document that said she would never write about her experiences.

Dorothy never achieved her dream of being a war correspondent, but in 1919, despite warnings, she wrote her autobiography and shared her exploits with the world, thus cracking the door open for future female war correspondents who would follow in her footsteps.

CATHERINE LEROY

FABULOUS PHOTOGRAPHER

Catherine grew up in the suburbs of Paris and was a small, sickly child. She suffered from severe asthma, and her parents didn't approve of her being active. Instead, she stayed inside, played the piano, and read books, magazines, and newspapers.

Besides being frail, she was also stubborn and was always looking for a new and exciting adventure.

It didn't take much coaxing from her boyfriend to try parachuting. She loved it, and by age eighteen, she'd earned her parachutist's license with over eighty jumps. This skill would come in handy later in her career.

The French magazine *Paris Match* sparked her interest in photography with its authentic, emotional, and heartbreaking images of the war in Vietnam.

In 1966, when she was only twenty-one years old, Catherine made a bold decision. With a hundred dollars and no return ticket, she packed her camera and made her way to South Vietnam intending to "give war a human face."

She convinced the Associated Press to hire her as a freelance photographer and was paid fifteen dollars per photo. It was not an easy task because women had been banned from being on the front lines of battle. But since it hadn't been officially declared a war and was officially called a "conflict," she wasn't breaking the law, just decades of assumptions that women couldn't handle the horrors of war.

Since she was so petite, the army didn't stock combat boots in her small size, so she had to buy them herself from street vendors at her own expense. Catherine taught herself English, lived, ate, and traveled from troop to troop. She wasn't treated differently and was expected to carry her own pack—which often weighed as much as she did.

Catherine was the first accredited photojournalist to participate in a combat parachute jump in 1967. She was the only one with prior parachuting experience. She had to be weighted down for the jump to keep her from blowing away.

The troops got used to her quietly being by their side, and she captured on film the loneliness, horror, stress, and gut-wrenching sorrow of battle that was reflected in their eyes and expressions.

Catherine was severely injured by mortar fire and suffered multiple shrapnel wounds and a fractured jaw. After recovering, she went back to the front lines and continued taking photographs, which were sold to more media outlets and brought the images of war directly into the hands and hearts of readers all around the world.

1953- UNITED STATES

MARGARET "MEG" LOWMAN

* AVID ARBORNAUT *

As a child, Meg was happiest outside climbing trees, picking wildflowers, observing insects, building forts in the forest, and especially bird-watching.

Other kids didn't share her passion, so she joined the local Audubon Society. She was their youngest member—by several decades! Luckily, she found a place where she belonged—a nature study camp in West Virginia where she spent several summers with like-minded nature lovers.

Meg was one of a handful of women who studied science in college, and when she was offered a fellowship to study the Australian rainforests, she was one of only two female PhD students. Not all professors believed women should be in the field, but her passion and devotion helped her overcome prejudice to become one of the first arbornauts—or treetop scientists.

Other scientists had studied the rainforest at eye level, but no one had studied it from the *top* because it was impossible to reach.

Or was it?

Meg was determined to find a way!

She used climbing gear, ropes, and a harness she made out of seat belt straps to construct a single-rope climbing system. At first, she often found herself twisting, turning, and flipping upside down high above the ground. The more she practiced, the easier it became, and soon she was studying the tree canopy up close and personal. But she realized that most of the animal activity happened at night, and she needed to create a safer system.

So, she built a walkway through the trees with ladders and ropes! It was successful, but Meg still wanted to go even higher and look at the canopy from above. With the help of a team of scientists in Africa, they devised a way for a hot-air balloon to situate a platform on the treetops. Now, they could look down on the amazing rainforest! Meg's passion for the rainforest grew with this amazing bird's-eye view. And so did her concern for its welfare.

Meg became an avid advocate for the protection and conservation of rainforests. She shared her knowledge of their importance through lectures, webinars, and tours. Meg hosted live satellite talks to thousands of students all around the world. She encouraged them to learn more about rainforests all they could about the natural world around them.

KATHRIN BARBOZA MARQUEZ

BRAVE BIOLOGIST

When Kathrin was in college in Bolivia studying biology with an emphasis on conservation, she happened to lose a bet with her friends. Her punishment? To attend a lecture on bats from a visiting professor and bat expert.

She didn't know much about these nocturnal mammals—only that many people saw them as scary or annoying.

But a bet was a bet, so she reluctantly went to the lecture.

And it changed her life!

Kathrin was amazed to learn how important bats are in providing natural pest control for hundreds of fruits. And how they are a crucial element in plant pollination. And that there are over 1,300 different and fascinating species.

Her interest in conservation now had a new focus—to study and protect bats.

In 2006, she embarked on a yearlong expedition in Bolivia to seek out and study bats. She'd be examining them, tagging wings, taking notes, and making maps. Conditions were less than ideal. It was grueling. Exhausting. Both mentally and physically challenging. At times Kathrin wondered if it was worth it.

But then she spotted a Tomes's sword-nosed bat. A bat that had been considered *extinct* for over seventy years! Obviously, it was still alive and well! And Kathrin was determined to keep it that way. After this amazing discovery, Latin America did something for the first time—they designated the area a protected sanctuary for this species of bats.

Kathrin continued her research on bats and in 2010 won the National Geographic Young Explorers Grant. She focused on how bats communicate with one another by emitting ultrasonic pulses that bounce off an object and return. She helped create a library of their echolocation frequencies that scientists and researchers use to expand their knowledge of how bats navigate their world and "talk" to each other.

In 2013, the BBC named her one of the ten leading female scientists in Latin America. Kathrin continues to research, learn, educate, and encourage girls to participate in conservation and pursue careers in science.

She's incredibly accomplished for someone who found her life's passion and career path after losing a bet!

And she's just getting started!

Bolivia
La Paz

IDA PFEIFFER

* EXTRAORDINARY EXPLORER *

Ida's father disagreed with the norm that boys should be educated and girls should be taught domestic pursuits. Instead, he encouraged her to study alongside her brothers, play sports, and explore the countryside. A family trip to Egypt when she was five sparked a lifelong love of traveling.

She was encouraged to marry a much older man, and for twenty-seven years she appeared to be simply a devoted wife and mother to two sons, her wanderlust set aside. But secretly, she read travel books and studied geography.

When she became widowed in her forties, her sons were living on her own, and she received a small inheritance from her mother. Nothing could hold her back, and off she went to see the world!

She sailed across the Black Sea, rode a camel through Egypt, and stopped at several countries on her way back to Vienna. Along the way she kept detailed notes of the places, scenery, culture, and people she met.

One trip wasn't enough. To pay for her next adventure, she published her travel journals, and they were bestsellers!

Her next trip wasn't just about sightseeing. This time she traveled to Scandinavia and Iceland and collected and preserved plant specimens, rocks, and minerals. She even climbed a volcano!

Where to go next? Around the world! She visited temples in Hong Kong, explored ancient ruins, and again took detailed notes of her adventures. If there wasn't a bed, she'd sleep on the ground or in a barn, never afraid or worried about harsh conditions—she just wanted to see the world.

Ida carefully collected over seven hundred specimens of preserved insects, seaweed, plants, marine life, birds, rocks, and minerals from around the globe.

When it was time to finance her next trip around the world, she sold her specimens to the Imperial Natural History Museum of Austria-Hungary. This time she traveled with scientists, paleontologists, and naturalists after having proved herself worthy of accompanying such an elite group of researchers.

Upon her return to Vienna, she published more travel journals that were translated into seven languages. Her amazing exploits were written about in a popular magazine—accompanied by a photo of her in her practical travel costume while holding a butterfly net and specimen bag.

Ida was a fearless explorer who inspired other women to follow their own adventurous spirit—no matter where it might take them.

MIRIAM ROTHSCHILD

* ECCENTRIC ENTOMOLOGIST *

Miriam was born into the wealthy Rothschild banking family, and her childhood was anything but ordinary!

They lived in an enormous mansion with a yard filled with flower gardens and trees. And wandering zebras, tortoises, and kangaroos!

Her father didn't believe in formal education, so the natural world became Miriam's classroom. By four years old, she was collecting and studying ladybugs, caterpillars, and other insects. She was fascinated by birds and had a pet quail that slept in bed with her.

Two years after her father died when she was fifteen years old, Miriam insisted on attending zoology classes at Chelsea College of Science and Technology. She focused her attention on her favorite species—FLEAS!

She spent over two years studying how fleas jumped and was the first person to prove they could jump up to ten inches.

Miriam married and had children but continued to study, collect, and observe. After the children went to bed, she went to her microscope and continued her work as an entomologist. She even kept fleas in a cellophane bag in her bedroom so she could watch them during the night.

Over the years, she observed over two thousand different types of fleas, carefully documenting her research.

During World War II, her attention turned to helping others. She opened her home to Jewish refugees and took in dozens of children. Then her home became a Red Cross hospital while she worked on a top secret project decoding enemy messages.

When the war ended, she realized her home had been ransacked and left in shambles. The beautiful gardens were now wild and overgrown. Weeds and ivy covered the once carefully manicured lawns.

Instead of returning the grounds to their original pristine state, she realized the abundance of wildflowers were helping to revive the diminishing butterfly population. Miriam eventually grew over one hundred species of wildflowers on what she called her "ex-lawns." She carefully collected the seeds by hand, and packaged and sold them—encouraging others to create butterfly and wildflower gardens throughout the English countryside. Her philosophy was that if the natural world could be preserved, it could also be created with a little help from farmers, gardeners, and nature lovers.

Between her fondness for fleas, strong views of conservation, and the "natural state of her home," many called her "eccentric" or worse. Yet, scientists and researchers included her in academic discussions, and she lectured at several colleges. Miriam shared her vast knowledge with others by writing over three hundred scientific papers and fifteen books.

Eccentric? Maybe. An incredible entomologist? Absolutely!

ARUNIMA SINHA

* TRIUMPH OVER TRAGEDY *

As a child, Arunima loved being active—bicycling, playing soccer and volleyball. After studying law in college, she hoped to work in law enforcement.

But then tragedy struck. On April 11, 2011, Arunima was on a train to Delhi when she was attacked by thieves. They wanted her gold necklace. She refused to give it to them and fought back. They overpowered her and threw her off the moving train.

After hitting another train, landing on the tracks, and being run over, she was barely clinging to life. After spending the night on the tracks, she was finally taken to an ill-equipped hospital later the next day.

Her left leg was amputated—while she was still awake. A steel rod was placed in her right leg from her ankle to her knee.

Recovery was slow and painful—but even before she was fitted with a prosthetic leg, she had made a bold decision. Not only would she walk again, but she would also climb a mountain. And not just any mountain, but Mount Everest!

Everyone thought it was an absolutely unattainable goal.

Everyone, except Arunima.

When Arunima was released from the hospital she began mountaineer training—every day for eighteen months. It was excruciating and exhausting. She scaled a few smaller mountains and sustained more injuries. But Arunima refused to give up. Her determination knew no bounds.

Finally, on April 1, 2013, Arunima started her journey up Mount Everest. For fifty-two days, she ignored the pain and danger and kept climbing. Finally, she reached the summit! Proudly she planted the flag of India. She called it the "best day of my life."

But climbing down Mount Everest can be even more treacherous than climbing up. She was exhausted, suffocating and gasping for breath when she found an extra cylinder of oxygen, cheating death once again.

Arunima wasn't content to be the first female amputee to climb Mount Everest. She had a new goal—to scale the highest mountain peaks on all seven continents.

And she did!

It was an astonishing accomplishment for someone who had to relearn to walk after a horrific ordeal.

Arunima now runs a nonprofit sports academy for underprivileged, handicapped children. She helps them gain the strength and confidence to achieve their goals—just like she did.

MADGE SYERS

SKILLFUL SKATER

Being one of fifteen children, Madge always had plenty of playmates! They were an athletic and active bunch who enjoyed swimming, horseback riding, and in the winter months—ice-skating.

During the Victorian era, figure skating was literally the ability to skate in figures—like the number eight or circles. As the sport gained in popularity, it evolved into a more creative and artistic style that incorporated graceful dance moves, spins, and jumps.

It wasn't long before it became a competitive sport, and in 1896, the first World Figure Skating Championship was held. All the participants were men because it never occurred to anyone that a *woman* might want to compete.

Until Madge skated onto the scene.

She entered the 1903 World Championship competition, which was held in London.

People were shocked! Scandalized! There had to be a rule forbidding women from skating competitively, right?

Wrong.

It had never occurred to anyone that a woman might want to enter when the rules were adopted, so there was no explicit rule forbidding it.

Madge used that to her advantage and entered the competition. At that time, skating outfits weren't sparkly form-fitting leotards like they are today. Instead, Madge wore a long, heavy black skirt, a satin shirt, a string of pearls, and a jaunty hat!

And she won the silver medal, placing second out of the four skaters—the others being men since there was no women's division.

Her victory caused a public outcry and the International Skating Union held meetings to debate the issue of female competitors.

After many heated discussions, they voted to ban women from all competitive figure skating. One of their reasons was that a woman's long skirt covered her ankles so judges couldn't see their fancy footwork accurately.

Madge had an easy solution—she simply raised her skirt to mid-calf! She bravely entered more figure skating championships—and continued to win, dazzling both the judges and spectators with her grace and ability. She was one of the first skaters to perform technical and flawless jumps in her routine.

Figure skating was added to the Olympic Games for the first time in 1908. Madge entered and easily won the gold medal—opening the door for future generations of female ice-skaters.

HELEN THAYER

* INTREPID EXPLORER *

Helen grew up on a sheep and cattle ranch and loved being outside. As a child, she wanted to climb Mount Taranaki with her parents, so she trained every day by walking the two miles to school and back—in the snow.

And she accomplished that goal when she was nine years old, sparking a lifelong passion for adventure.

While in school, she excelled at sports and became a world-class discus thrower and a luge sledding champion. But early on, she decided she would set and achieve personal goals rather than compete against others.

Over the years, she climbed many more mountains, kayaked the Amazon River, traveled to dozens of countries, and searched for her next grand venture.

In 1988, she had a new goal—to be the first woman to hike to the magnetic North Pole. Alone.

She packed a seven-foot sled with 160 pounds of supplies and set out, accompanied by her dog Charlie. He'd pull his own sled filled with eighty-five pounds of dog food. He wasn't just a companion; he was there to chase away polar bears! And they met several along the way.

The duo also encountered ice storms and frigid temperatures that injured her fingers, causing excruciating pain and making even simple tasks almost impossible. Yet, Helen trekked on. When she got close to the magnetic North Pole, her compass no longer worked, and she had to navigate with a sundial.

Finally, success! But it would take seven more days living on a handful of walnuts and sips of water as she hiked to the pickup spot when a plane would retrieve her.

And her adventures continued!

In 1994, Helen, her husband, and dog Charlie hiked to the Arctic Circle and lived near a wolf den for six months to study and document the daily activities of wolves which she wrote about in her book *Three Among the Wolves*.

In 1996, she tackled a different climate and became the first woman to hike across the Sahara Desert. A year later, it was back to the Arctic where she celebrated her sixtieth birthday on the Polar ice cap with a frozen cupcake.

But Helen wasn't done. In 2001, at sixty-three years old, Helen crossed Mongolia's Gobi Desert accompanied by her husband and two camels. Still recovering from severe injuries sustained in a car accident, she limped over 1,600 miles in scorching heat amid sandstorms and scorpions.

In 2002, she was named one of the Great Explorers of the Twentieth Century by National Geographic—an honor she so richly deserved.

JEANNE VILLEPREUX-POWER

* MARVELOUS MARINE BIOLOGIST *

Over two hundred years ago in France, a seamstress and shoemaker had a daughter they named Jeanne. As a young woman she followed in their footsteps and became a hatmaker and seamstress. She moved to Paris and continued snipping fabric and sewing seams. Until she met her soon-to-be husband who whisked her off to live in Sicily.

Jeanne had never seen an ocean and she fell instantly in love! She scoured the countryside and shores of her new home collecting shells, plants, and rocks and making detailed sketches of everything she saw.

What fascinated her the most were the creatures that lived in the sea. At that time, scientists could only study them when they were dead. That wasn't good enough for Jeanne. But what could she do about it?

In 1832, with some wood and glass, Jeanne built something nobody had ever seen before—an aquarium! She joined forces with local fishermen to catch fish, snails, slugs, starfish—and her favorite—octopuses. Now she could bring these amazing creatures into her home and observe them daily!

But what about larger species that live in much deeper water? Or ones she wanted to study in their natural habitat? No problem! Jeanne built a glass cage that could be lowered and raised to observe those hard-to-catch species. And another one that was anchored to the seabed in shallow water. Years later, the Zoological Society of London called them "power cages" after their intrepid inventor.

After studying marine life in her aquariums, she turned her attention to a mystery that had baffled scientists for decades. A unique species of octopus called an argonaut lived in a shell. But where did the shell come from? Did they move into an abandoned one like a hermit crab? Or did they somehow build their own shell?

Jeanne was determined to solve the riddle!

She collected argonaut eggs from the sea and watched them carefully in her aquarium. After a few days she saw them creating their own shell through the wonders of biochemistry. No need to borrow a used shell. Mystery solved!

Throughout her lifetime, Jeanne made many astonishing discoveries—including that octopus are amazingly intelligent creatures. She wrote books, scientific papers, and made detailed drawings of her conclusions and inspired generations of scientists to study, learn, and protect the marine life she loved.

Greetings from
WYOMING
Greetings from
ARKANSAS
Greetings from
TENNESSEE

ANNIE WILKINS

TRUSTING TRAVELER

Annie's life in Maine had never been easy. She dropped out of school when she was only twelve years old to work in a shoe factory. Her family barely eked out a living on their farm. After two failed marriages, the loss of all family members, and no savings, sixty-three-year-old Annie got more bad news. Her doctor said she only had a few years to live. He suggested she move into a charity home where she could get some much-needed rest.

Annie disagreed. Instead, she decided to do something she'd dreamt about since she was a child—go to California and see the Pacific Ocean. Getting there wouldn't be easy, but Annie was determined.

To raise money for her adventure, she grew one more crop before she lost the farm to back taxes. She harvested her cucumbers and made and sold jars of pickles, earning her thirty-two dollars. She bought an old racehorse named Tarzan whom she would ride across the country!

She packed light—a few tools, frying pan, canned food, and hay and grain for Tarzan. She wore several layers of clothes and with her dog Depeche Toi (French for "hurry up") trotting alongside, she set off.

Without cell phones or GPS, she relied on gas station maps to plan her route even though some were old and inaccurate. Annie believed in the goodness of others and hoped to find kind strangers along the way that would provide a warm bed and meals.

And that's exactly what happened!

Early on a reporter did a story on her. Then another reporter added to the story, this time with photographs. News of her trip spread across the country and soon townspeople were welcoming her and her four-legged traveling companions. Annie realized her journey had struck a chord with many people, and she was even more determined to get to California—for herself—and for everyone who didn't have the means to follow their dreams.

Annie encountered snowstorms, thunderstorms, stampeding cattle, poisonous snakes, a flash flood, desert heat, illness—and even one marriage proposal from a goat herder in Wyoming along the way. But she never gave up, no matter what she faced.

After riding through eighteen states, across thousands of miles for seventeen long months, Annie reached her destination—California and the Pacific Ocean—thanks to the outpouring of support and kindness of strangers—who became friends—along the way.

REBELS

ALICIA ALONSO

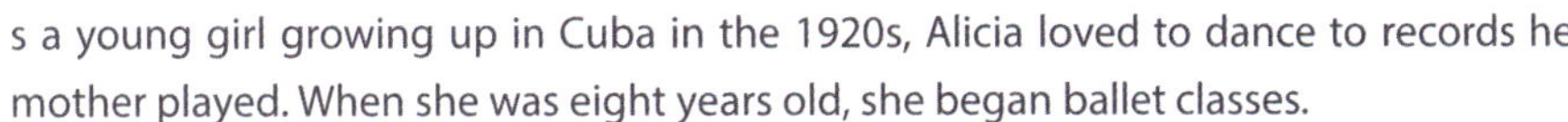

BRAVE BALLERINA

As a young girl growing up in Cuba in the 1920s, Alicia loved to dance to records her mother played. When she was eight years old, she began ballet classes.

Unfortunately, neither the dance school nor the students could afford much in the way of proper attire. Ballet is hard, and dancing in old tennis shoes and street clothes is even harder! But Alicia still loved her lessons.

When the school finally acquired *one* pair of ballerina pointe shoes, every single student tried them on. And they only fit Alicia so they became hers!

By sixteen, she had learned as much as the school could teach her, so she moved to New York to further her training at the School of American Ballet. Alicia worked hard to perfect her technique and skills. She was becoming an excellent ballerina!

But at nineteen, a problem arose. When Alicia was onstage, the lights seemed to dim. She began bumping into other dancers and losing her place. The theater lights were fine, but her eyesight wasn't. Alicia was slowly going blind.

Alicia had eye surgery, which meant months of recovery. Eyes bandaged, in bed, no moving. And certainly, no dancing.

So, Alicia rehearsed every movement, every step of a ballet in her head. And she stretched and pointed her toes to keep her legs limber.

Finally, the bandages came off. Alicia looked around. The surgery had *not* improved her vision.

She had two more eye surgeries.

Two more long recoveries.

And still no success.

Alicia refused to give up dancing. But how could a ballerina with limited eyesight perform? She was determined to figure it out!

Alicia worked with her partners so they would always be in the same position. She carefully counted her steps, concentrated on the music, and had spotlights shining directly on her to help her know she was in the right position onstage.

She continued to dance—brilliantly! Alicia charmed audiences around the world and earned numerous awards and honors for her incredible talent.

Eventually, Alicia returned to Cuba and started her own renowned ballet school. She taught, encouraged, and inspired generations of dancers. She even continued to dazzle audiences with her solo performances into her seventies.

Alicia danced her way into people's hearts by her skill, dedication, and sheer determination to succeed—no matter what obstacles she faced along the way.

ETHELDA BLEIBTREY

SASSY SWIMMER

In the early 1900s, girls were encouraged to only play nonstrenuous sports like croquet or lawn tennis. Ethelda was a weak and frail child suffering from polio and her doctor persuaded her to take up the unladylike activity of swimming to help strengthen her muscles and increase her stamina.

And she loved it! At sixteen, she joined the Women's Swimming Association, which held races and competitions around the country. Ethelda excelled in pools, ponds, lakes, and even the Atlantic Ocean. She was a champion in both short and long distances—and in any type of stroke.

When she was seventeen, she went for a swim at New York's Manhattan Beach and caused such a commotion that the police were summoned. They came and arrested her.

The charge?

Public nudity!

Had Ethelda been skinny-dipping?

Nope.

She had merely removed her *socks* before entering the water!

The public outcry kept her out of jail and convinced lawmakers to loosen the strict and ridiculous "rules" for female swimmers and sunbathers.

Fashion wasn't the only "rule" she believed was outdated. At that time, women's hair was expected to be long. So, Ethelda had hers cut into a short, sassy bob!

Her next challenge was the 1920 Olympics in Antwerp, Belgium. She entered all the women's swimming events. All three of them.

They swam outside in the cold. The pool had no lanes and no blocks. As the starting gun fired, they dove in and swam, trying not to bump into each other.

Ethelda won gold—in all three events. She was the first woman from the United States to win an Olympic gold medal in a swimming event. And she continued to swim and win in more races over the next several years.

Her attention then turned to helping others. Ethelda gave swimming lessons to children with disabilities. But there weren't many pools in New York. There *was* the Central Park Reservoir, although swimming wasn't allowed due to a city ordinance.

She dove in. The police were summoned, and she was arrested. Once again, the public was outraged! The mayor got involved, and she was released from jail. More importantly, New York then built its first public swimming pool.

In 1967, Ethelda was inducted into the International Swimming Hall of Fame. Her accomplishments in the water are legendary, and so was her determination to fight for women's rights.

59
13

MARGARET CHUNG

DEVOTED DOCTOR

Margaret was the eldest of eleven children born to Chinese immigrant parents. Her parents were often ill, so she stepped up to care for and support the whole family—before she was a teenager.

She watched as the local doctor rode his bicycle from house to house and dreamt that one day, she would also become a doctor.

It wasn't going to be easy, but Margaret was determined. With no savings to pay for college, she relied on scholarship money from the *Los Angeles Times* for selling newspaper subscriptions. She also won prize money from speech contests and waitressing at night after classes.

She was the only woman in class but didn't let that keep her from excelling. In 1916, she became the first female Chinese American physician. But finding a job was difficult. She was turned down when she applied to be a medical missionary to China and again as a surgical nurse in Los Angeles.

Margaret moved to Chicago for two years and worked in psychiatry. Then she returned to California to be closer to her family. In 1922, she opened her practice in San Francisco's Chinatown where she had an interesting group of patients. She catered to many Hollywood movie stars, locals, and Navy Reserve pilots!

During WWII, Margaret's small group of pilot patients grew to include over a thousand military members who lovingly called her "Mom Chung." She considered them to be her "adopted children" and wrote uplifting letters and sent them morale-boosting care packages. On Sunday nights, she cooked dinner for any servicemen in the area.

Margaret volunteered to be a battle surgeon on the front lines but instead was asked to recruit pilots for the Flying Tigers unit. She kept track of each one of them, wrote letters, and taped their replies to her office walls. She continued to host dinners for military members and sent over four thousand wrapped Christmas presents to troops overseas.

Margaret held an unpopular belief at the time—that women should be allowed to join the military. She helped introduce legislation to create the WAVES (Women Accepted for Volunteer Emergency Services) organization. In 1942, the law passed to allow women to join the Reserve Corps of the Navy.

Margaret refused to let racial or gender biases keep her from achieving her dream of becoming a physician, substitute mother, and advocate for women's rights.

KATHLEEN "KIT" COLEMAN

* REBEL REPORTER *

Kit was a curious and inquisitive child, and her father encouraged her love of reading, learning, and exploration. Her mother passed along her appreciation of music, and Kit learned to play several instruments.

She immigrated to Canada to pursue her dream of becoming a journalist. The *Toronto Mail* hired her to write a column called the Woman's Kingdom. It contained recipes, housekeeping tips, and advice to the lovelorn. These were NOT the topics Kit was interested in! So she occasionally added items about politics, business ventures, and social reform.

She became restless and convinced her editor to explore investigative journalism, under the byline Kit Coleman. She covered high-profile court cases, giving readers a front-row seat to the biggest scandals of the day. Kit also traveled to other countries, writing about her adventures. Before long she'd earned a reputation as an international star reporter with worldwide fans.

In 1898, the Spanish–American War began, and Kit had a new goal—to report from Cuba's front lines. At first her male editors were horrified! A woman on a battlefield? Ridiculous! Kit persisted and finally they relented, but told her she could only write "soft stories" about what happened behind the scenes, far removed from the actual fighting.

Even with their approval, she met obstacles. The United States didn't allow female journalists, so she went to Washington, DC, and convinced the secretary of war to issue her war correspondent accreditation—the first woman ever to receive it.

Getting to Cuba was another problem. She spent six weeks in Florida while military officers refused to let her board a troop ship. Finally, Kit made it to the front lines and wrote about the trauma and devastation of war on the soldiers, their families, and the countries involved. She wrote from a different perspective than her male colleagues and showed the human side of war. Readers were enthralled by her personal accounts, and she earned worldwide acclaim.

Back home in Canada, Kit faced a new battle—discrimination. She wasn't allowed to join press clubs because she was a woman. So, in 1906, she helped create the Canadian Women's Press Club.

In 1911, she asked the newspaper to pay her the same wages as the male journalists. They refused. She quit—and became the first syndicated female columnist in Canada.

With courage and persistence, Kit paved the way for generations of future female journalists.

WOMANS

3-6-9 KID
3-6-9 KID

AGNES DALUGE

* SPECTACULAR SPY *

Agnes grew up in poverty where food and medical care were scarce, which caused several life-threatening illnesses and infections as a child. When she was well enough, she loved attending the one-room schoolhouse in her only blue-and-gray dress.

When she was eleven, her declining health was so dire, she moved to Germany to live with her Aunt Rosa where she could have a healthier diet and much-needed medical care. She thrived but remained petite and frail—looking like someone half her age.

And that became an asset for the dangerous path her life would take!

Agnes was intelligent and had a knack for memorization, which helped her become fluent in German very quickly. When she was twelve years old, her aunt sent to London where Agnes was tutored in English and attended school to help her become even more proficient.

Agnes was aware that World War II was spreading across western Europe but was encouraged not to ask questions. Her aunt was always busy and secretive, but Agnes didn't know what was really going on—she was happy with the bountiful meals, clean clothes, and string of tutors.

In 1941, she was sent to Paris for five months to learn French! Soon fluent in several languages, she returned to Aunt Rosa's house and was asked to translate letters from German to English for Rosa's "visitors." This young schoolgirl was now working undercover to help Jews escape Nazi Germany.

Agnes was frequently memorizing precise codes that she would pass onto others in the spy network. Nobody expected such a young, tiny girl to be doing such dangerous work, so her first code name was 3-6-9 KID!

She wasn't paid for her work but was promised American citizenship after the war—if she survived.

On her fifteenth birthday she received a strange gift—an accordion—with a special purpose. She took lessons for her most daring mission—out in the open. She played at recitals with secret agents in the audience. She'd smile as she hit a note that revealed a coded message and did it successfully over twenty times!

Agnes frequently spent time at Rosa's vacation villa where she hid Jewish refugees and POWs in a secret underground room before they hiked over the mountains into Switzerland—and freedom.

Because of her courage and bravery, hundreds of lives were saved by the spy nicknamed "mighty mouse."

MICHAELA DEPRINCE

GROUNDBREAKING BALLERINA

Michaela's early years weren't easy. She was born during a brutal civil war and had vitiligo—a skin condition that caused numerous spots. Children were cruel and even relatives called her "devil's child."

Her parents were loving and admired her drive and curiosity. She picked up several languages at the local market and learned to read at a young age.

When she was only three years old, her father was killed, and shortly thereafter, her mother died.

Michaela was alone. And unwanted by her uncle. He tossed her into the back of his truck, took her to an orphanage, and left her.

The children were given numbers. Number one was the favorite and most likely to be adopted. Michaela was number twenty-seven out of twenty-seven and considered to have the least chance of being adopted.

She made friends with Number Twenty-Six—who was ostracized because she was left-handed. But others ignored them both, and Michaela was once again called hurtful names.

Michaela wanted to be friends with everyone, so she suggested they all play a game she'd made up. Reluctant at first, they soon joined in. And begged her every morning to make up a new game to play!

One day she found the glossy cover of an old magazine that had blown against the orphanage's gate. Michaela was mesmerized by the beautiful woman's graceful pose in a tutu.

She didn't know what a ballerina was. She didn't even know what dancing was. But she decided right then and there she wanted to be just like that woman.

Soon, both Michaela and her friend were adopted by the same family in New Jersey. It was the beginning of a whole new life—a life that included ballet lessons!

Michaela LOVED anything related to dance. She bought a used copy of *The Nutcracker* and practiced the routines. When she was thirteen, she went to a ballet boarding school, practicing many hours a day, every day.

Soon she was winning competitions and being offered scholarships. Her career soared and she was doing what she'd always dreamt of—being a ballerina onstage.

Through some internet sleuthing and some help from *Dance Magazine*, Michaela discovered the model on that ragged magazine was ballerina Magali Messac. She was able to thank her for inspiring her to follow her dream of dancing, and Michaela has also inspired children worldwide to follow their dreams.

ADMIT ONE
NOV 8th 1946
ADMIT ONE
NOV 8th 1946

VIOLA DESMOND

* PEACEFUL PROTESTOR *

Viola's father was a barber, which may have been what sparked her interest in hair and skin care. She wanted to become a beautician, but opportunities to train were limited for Black women in Halifax at that time.

So, Viola traveled and studied at beauty schools in Montreal, Atlantic City, and New York. She returned to Halifax and opened her own salon—Vi's Studio of Beauty Culture.

But she was just getting started! Knowing how hard it had been to get proper training, she created a school to teach other budding Black beauticians. After graduating, she helped them start their own salons.

Next, she started selling her own line of beauty products. It was on one of these sales trips to Nova Scotia that changed Viola's life. On November 8, 1946, her car broke down and she was told it could take hours to repair. No problem—there was a nearby movie theater where she could spend the afternoon.

She bought a ticket and found a seat on the main floor, near the screen for the best view. But then she was told she had to move to the balcony simply because she was Black. Viola politely refused and offered to pay an additional cost to stay where she was. After all, she just wanted to watch a movie!

The theater manager called the police. They came and dragged her out of the theater—injuring her hip and knee. She was charged with attempting to defraud the government by sitting in the main section (which was for whites only) rather than paying one penny more for a balcony seat. She offered to pay the penny. The judge refused and fined her twenty-six dollars!

A reporter broke the story and there was a public outcry. Viola hired a lawyer, and the case went to court. Instead of focusing on the blatant discrimination, the government said the case was really about that one-cent tax.

Viola lost the case. But she won the hearts of the public. Newspapers and magazines wrote about the injustice of her ordeal. A grassroots movement formed to fight discrimination and racial prejudice in Canada.

For her quiet determination and peaceful protest, she was honored many times after her death—even appearing on Canadian currency. All because she refused to change seats—eight years before Rosa Parks did the same thing on a bus in the United States.

FLORENCE FINCH

Florence grew up in an abusive and unhappy home. She found comfort and solace in books and her own imagination. When she was only seven years old, she was sent to boarding school in Manila.

The school kept to a strict schedule of classes, exercise, and chores. Florence was overwhelmed at first but soon fell in love with the routines. She was a model student and earned perfect grades.

After graduating, she took business classes and was hired as a stenographer in the Office of Army Intelligence in Manila. She met and married an American soldier.

Then tragedy struck—Pearl Harbor was attacked, and the United States entered World War II. Six months later, her husband was killed, and Florence vowed to do whatever she could for the war effort.

Her mother had been Filipino and her father American—a fact she hid from the occupying forces. With her beautiful penmanship, she earned a job filling out gas ration coupons. But she had an ulterior motive—she worked with the Philippine resistance movement and forged coupons diverting supplies to underground couriers who sold the supplies on the black market. Money raised was used to buy food, clothing, and medical supplies for American prisoners of war. Prison guards allowed packages to be sent to the men because then they wouldn't have to feed or care for the wounded.

Florence continued her dangerous work, forging coupons and falsifying documents.

Then the unthinkable happened. She was caught and tortured, but she refused to give up the names of her coconspirators. Sentenced to three years of hard labor, she toiled in the hot sun, losing weight and growing weaker by the day.

On February 10, 1945, American troops marched into the prison, and she was freed! She regained her strength and moved to New York to live with relatives.

Florence had gone above and beyond, risking her own life to aid others during wartime. But she wasn't done!

She enlisted in the U.S. Coast Guard Women's Reserve and continued to serve. Florence didn't speak of her activities during the war, so when news broke of her work during the resistance, friends and family were shocked but not surprised. Florence had always done whatever she could to help others.

Florence was awarded the American Medal of Freedom. And in 1995, the Coast Guard named their new Pacific headquarters after her for her heroism, courage, and the hundreds of lives she saved.

UNITED STATES COAST GUARD
1790
UNITED STATES COAST GUARD
1790
RATION
RATION

NATIONAL AUDUBON SOCIETY
1.00
NATIONAL AUDUBON SOCIETY
1.00
1.00
NATIONALAUDUBON SOCIETY
1.00
NATIONALAUDUBON SOCIETY

HARRIET HEMENWAY

* BIRD BENEFACTOR *

Harriet was a fan of fashion—gorgeous gowns, sparkling jewelry, and sassy shoes. And every outfit needed a fancy hat adorned with beads, ribbons, and feathers. The bigger and brighter the feathers, the better!

She hadn't given a thought to where those fantastic feathers came from until one day she read an article in the *Boston Daily Globe.* It was about birds—millions of birds—who were killed for their feathers. From pigeons and peacocks; to herons and hummingbirds. She was horrified!

Harriet would never wear a feather again. But she needed to do more. How could she convince other women to give them up?

Harriet shared what she'd learned with her cousin Minna Hall and the two joined forces. Together they hatched a plan to spread the word. They would invite all their fashionable friends to a tea party—and explain why they should stop using feathers for decoration.

Some listened and swore to give up their feathered hats. Others weren't persuaded.

At least, not yet.

More determined than ever, Harriet contacted bird experts and held lectures on the importance of protecting birds.

And she hosted more tea parties.

Many women wanted to get involved, so Harriet founded the Massachusetts Audubon Society, named after the famous bird artist. But women didn't hold much political power at that time—they weren't even allowed to vote! So, she enlisted the aid of New England's highly respected bird experts called ornithologists. Prominent men now flocked to take up the cause. It was no longer seen as a fashion issue but an important conservation issue. The group that started with a tea party now had almost one thousand members!

Word of her campaign to halt the use of bird feathers reached England and Queen Victoria herself vowed to never wear a feathered hat again!

Word kept spreading. And in 1897, a law was passed that made it illegal to buy or sell wild bird feathers. There was still a long way to go, but it was a great start.

Harriet's regional group expanded into the National Audubon Society, which now has millions of members that work on laws to protect and preserve wildlife habitats.

Harriet certainly deserves a feather in her cap—an *artificial* feather!

JULIA BUTTERFLY HILL

RESPECT YOUR ELDERS

* EPIC ENVIRONMENTALIST *

RESPECT YOUR ELDERS

Julia's father was a traveling preacher and her family lived in a camping trailer, moving from place to place. While hiking one day, a butterfly landed on her finger—and stayed—earning her the nickname "Butterfly."

When she was twenty-two years old, she was in a near-fatal car accident and suffered a traumatic brain injury. She spent the next year focusing on her recovery and rehabilitation—learning to walk and talk again.

Julia wasn't sure what to do next, so she joined a group of friends on a trip to the West Coast. When she first walked into a forest of ancient redwoods, she was simply awestruck and felt an overwhelming sense of peace and belonging. But she soon realized that a clear-cut logging company had started removing trees, causing a horrific mudslide that destroyed homes and displaced families.

Julia was outraged and wanted to do something to protect the redwoods. But what?

The answer was to join with others in a "tree-sit." They would live on a platform in a one thousand-year-old tree named Luna, which would keep loggers at bay. And would hopefully raise awareness of the plight of redwoods and the harm of deforestation.

Tree-sitters came and went. But Julia stayed. She refused to come down until Luna was spared. That meant living on oatmeal, dried fruit, and vegetables, sleeping under a tarp in all types of weather, and being alone for days at a time.

Julia endured rain, sleet, hail, and terrifying windstorms. During two harsh winters, she suffered from frostbite.

In nice weather, Julia scampered about the tree barefoot, without any safety ropes. She shared her tree home with flying squirrels, mice, bugs, and birds.

On her twenty-fourth birthday, the media took notice and her story appeared in magazines and newspapers. The public was now paying attention to the environmental concerns of the redwoods—and so was the logging company. Negotiations began—she'd come down if they would create a three-acre buffer zone around Luna. After months of discussions, more media coverage, and public support, an agreement was struck.

On December 18, 1999, after 738 days of living on Luna, Julia climbed down and stood next to the tree she had helped save.

Julia continues to advocate for environmental concerns and encourages others to get involved—because as she has proven, one person *can* make a difference.

RESPECT
YOUR
ELDERS

20
20
20
Clowns
Clowns

MAMIE "PEANUT" JOHNSON

POWERFUL PITCHER

When Mamie was a young girl, she played sandlot baseball with the neighborhood boys. The southern sun was hot, the makeshift field was dusty, and the bases were made of whatever they could find.

And she loved it.

When she wasn't in a game, she practiced pitching and batting—making her own balls out of twine-covered rocks.

Mamie dreamed of one day playing professional baseball. But that was a ridiculous dream for a young Black girl. Or was it?

One day she saw boys playing on a Police Athletic League. All boys. All white.

That didn't stop Mamie from asking the coach if she could try out. Surprisingly, he agreed.

And she amazed him and the other players with her pitching ability. Strike! Strike! Strike!

She earned a place on the team. And helped them win two division championships!

But Mamie wanted more. When she was seventeen years old, she tried out for the All-American Girls Professional Baseball League.

And was rejected. Because of the color of her skin.

She refused to give up. A year later, she tried out for the Indianapolis Clowns—a professional team in the Negro Leagues. Because of her petite size, she was nicknamed "Peanut." But it didn't bother her at all. She took her place on the mound and strike! Strike! Strike!

She made the team, and grudgingly, earned the other players' respect.

The team went from town to town in a crowded bus—sometimes playing double- and even triple-headers. It was exhausting, mentally and physically.

The press made it sound like a female pitcher was a gimmick. A curiosity. A way to lure fans into the bleachers. But when the fans saw Mamie in action—throwing fastballs, sliders, changeups, and her specialty, the curveball, and striking players out—they realized she *deserved* to be on the pitcher's mound.

Mamie was living her dream of playing professional baseball!

Years after she retired from baseball, she was given the honor of a Female Baseball Legend by President Clinton. She was honored again in 2013 by President Obama along with other Negro League players.

Mamie continued to coach and mentor young girls who loved baseball, encouraging them to follow their passion, just like she had.

When it came to achieving a dream, against all obstacles, Mamie "Peanut" Johnson hit one out of the park.

JENNIFER KEELAN-CHAFFINS

* DETERMINED DEMONSTRATOR *

When Jennifer was just a toddler, she learned that life wasn't always fair. Childhood was supposed to be a time for having fun, learning, and exploring new places.

But it wasn't always easy.

Jennifer was born with cerebral palsy—a condition that made walking difficult. A wheelchair gave her mobility. But society created roadblocks.

She couldn't ride a bus. Or go to libraries or museums because of the steps. Even her school was off-limits!

People with disabilities were tired of being denied access and treated unfairly. They banded together to voice their concerns. But was anyone listening?

Jennifer participated in her first protest when she was only six years old. People with all manner of disabilities wanted to be seen and treated as equals. She also worked with adults to help create the Americans with Disabilities Act (ADA)—which they hoped Congress would pass into law. That would mean buildings would have to be wheelchair accessible, curbs would have cutouts, and public transportation would have lifts, among other things. It meant fairness. Equality. And freedom.

The group planned a bold move. On March 12, 1990, they'd hold a "wheels of justice" march. People in wheelchairs would roll from the White House to the U.S. Capitol.

But the protest wouldn't end there. To demonstrate the need for access, they would leave their wheelchairs and crawl up the steps.

When eight-year-old Jennifer got to the Capitol, some of her fellow protestors encouraged her to stay in her wheelchair because of her size and young age.

She might have been small, but her determination to represent all children with disabilities was huge. Jennifer began crawling. The sun was hot. The eighty-three stone steps were hard. And steep.

Yet, Jennifer kept going. One step at a time.

Photographers snapped pictures. Reporters took notes. The group was finally being seen and heard. Their message was shared across the country. And people took notice.

Four months later, the ADA was signed into law. It was the largest bill-signing event in U.S. history at that time. Although a great accomplishment—there was still more work to be done. And Jennifer was up to the challenge. She continues to advocate for justice and equality for everyone—one step at a time.

Stop
Discrimination
NOW!!

Stop
Discrimination
NOW!!

VOTES FOR WOMEN
VOTES FOR WOMEN
VOTES for WOMEN

MABEL PING-HUA LEE

SUPERB SUFFRAGETTE

When Mabel was a child growing up in China, her father immigrated to the United States, and she was raised by her mother and grandmother. She attended a missionary school where she learned English and loved her classes. Due to her curiosity and excellent grades, she was awarded a scholarship, which allowed them to move to New York and reunite with her father.

Being exposed to two very different cultures gave Mabel a unique perspective and she realized something at an early age—that women did not have the same civil rights, voting rights, or equality in employment or wages. And she wanted to do what she could to change that!

She became an outspoken member of the suffragette movement. One of their biggest marches took place on May 4, 1912. Mabel was only sixteen years old yet led the group of ten thousand women through the streets of New York astride a white horse. She proudly wore a black hat and sash that said, "Votes for Women."

Six months later, another march was held—this time in the evening so working women could attend. They carried thousands of lanterns through the dark streets—lighting their way and shining a light on their cause.

Besides fighting for women's rights, her other passion was pursuing her education. She studied philosophy and history in college. Mabel was an active member of the debate club and wrote articles for student newspapers promoting equality for women.

In 1917, women won the right to vote in New York. Except for Mabel. Due to discrimination laws affecting Chinese immigrants at the time, she was not allowed to cast a ballot until 1943.

She continued her education, earning her bachelor's degree, and then a master's degree. But Mabel wasn't done! She received a PhD in economics from Columbia University—being the first Chinese American woman to do so.

After college, she traveled to Europe to study postwar economics. But her trip came to a halt when her father died, and she returned to New York to take over his ministry and look after her mother.

She raised funds to create a Chinese community center where English was taught along with secretarial skills, carpentry, and other vocational training. A medical clinic was added and then a kindergarten. Mabel devoted her life to improving the lives of women by fighting for their rights and equality.

VOTES FOR WOMEN

VOTES FOR WOMEN

MARTA

* SOCCER SUPERSTAR *

Marta Vieira da Silva grew up in a poverty-stricken neighborhood where every family member had to help. Instead of regularly attending school, she sold fruit in the market. When she did have spare time, she joined the boys in playing soccer in the streets.

She couldn't afford soccer shoes, so she played barefoot. No ball? No problem! Marta practiced with old deflated balls or made her own by tying plastic bags together. Nothing was going to keep her from the sport she loved.

Even though she endured taunting and teasing from the boys, her tenacity and sheer talent kept her from quitting. It wasn't just the boys that looked down on her for being athletic—so did adults. Girls in Brazil were *not* encouraged to play sports. Soccer was a national pastime, but women had been banned from playing from 1941–1979 because male politicians deemed the sport to be unfeminine. Even after the official ban had been lifted, participating in sports was *not* encouraged or promoted.

Marta wasn't discouraged by the negative comments from friends, family, and society. Instead, she worked harder to hone her skills.

And it paid off! When she was fourteen years old, a soccer coach happened to see her practice and was amazed by her talent and abilities. She convinced Marta to take the three-day bus trip to the tryouts for the Vasco da Gama women's soccer club. She made the team—the first step in her incredible career.

But there were more obstacles to overcome. Women's soccer wasn't as popular as men's soccer. Financial woes caused several leagues to disband—which meant moving to new teams—and new countries.

When Marta was seventeen years old, she moved to Sweden and dazzled the soccer world by winning the FIFA World Player of the Year Award FIVE years in a row! And she won a sixth time in 2018.

She also scored fifteen goals playing for Brazil in four World Cup Championships—a record that will be tough to beat! Added to that accomplishment were two Olympic silver medals.

Marta was appointed a United Nations Goodwill Ambassador and takes her position as a role model seriously to promote women's rights and equality in sports. She encourages children to pursue sports no matter their background.

She is considered to be the best female soccer player in the world and has brought worldwide attention and respect to the game she loves.

10
THE BEST
10
10
10

JENNIE SMILLIE ROBERTSON

* DETERMINED DOCTOR *

Jennie was only three years old when she met a female missionary doctor on her way to India—and decided she wanted to be a doctor when she grew up too! It was an ambitious dream for a farmer's daughter, but Jennie knew what she wanted.

When she was six, her father contracted tuberculosis and she watched as the local doctor cared for him before he died of the disease. This made Jennie even more determined to become a doctor and help those in need.

But it wouldn't be easy. Medical school was expensive, so Jennie received her teaching certificate and taught for seven years—saving as much of her three hundred-dollars-a-year salary as she could.

Finally, she could afford medical school! She studied hard and graduated in 1909. The next step was to intern in a hospital and further her education with hands-on experience. But not a single hospital in Canada would accept a female intern.

Undaunted, Jennie moved to Philadelphia, Pennsylvania, and attended the Women's Medical College. After graduating, she returned to Canada to embark on her next venture—training to become a surgeon. Alas, once again she was denied entry because she was a woman.

Back to the United States she went, where she trained under the supervision of a female surgeon.

Once again, she returned to Canada only to discover that no hospitals would hire a female surgeon or allow her to operate there.

No hospital for female surgeons? No problem! Jennie removed an ovarian tumor from a patient on her kitchen table! She was the first Canadian surgeon to perform major gynecological surgery.

By 1911, more and more female patients were seeking out female doctors and surgeons for their medical care. Jennie joined with other women in the field to open the Women's College Hospital. They didn't have a permanent building but rented out a house with beds for seven patients. Working with a shoestring budget, the founders gathered vegetables from local gardens to feed to their patients. The women also went door-to-door asking for donations, which allowed them to move to a bigger house and finally build a new hospital.

Jennie continued working as a doctor and surgeon until she was seventy years old. After devoting her life to medicine, she did something just for herself—she finally married her sweetheart!

Her determination and perseverance have inspired other girls and women to pursue medical careers—and to keep breaking down barriers.

DANIELA SOTO-INNES

* SHOWSTOPPING CHEF *

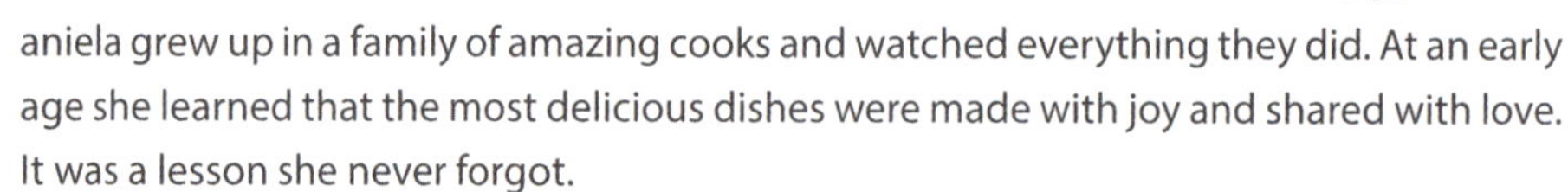

Daniela grew up in a family of amazing cooks and watched everything they did. At an early age she learned that the most delicious dishes were made with joy and shared with love. It was a lesson she never forgot.

Her grandmother owned a bakery, and by the time she was five years old, Daniela was taking after-school cooking classes! When she was twelve years old, the family moved from Mexico to Texas, and she cleverly merged traditional family recipes with new styles and ingredients.

Not realizing she was only fifteen, she was hired to work in the kitchen of a busy restaurant. She watched, listened, and learned—how to run a business and how NOT to treat your employees! She'd witnessed firsthand how some chefs bullied and berated their staff, insulted them, and created an unpleasant and hostile work environment. Daniela vowed that if she was ever in charge, she would treat her entire staff like family.

With her future career as a chef in mind, Daniela attended a technical school to focus on the culinary arts. She loved talking to other cooks and encouraging them to share the stories behind their favorite recipes. To her, personalities are as important as the ingredients!

When she achieved a goal of owning and running her own restaurants, she did it her way. She treats everyone as family and friends. The entire staff is encouraged to laugh, sing, and dance while preparing food because she knows the best food is cooked by happy, relaxed, and joyful cooks.

In 2016, when she was only twenty-five years old, Daniela received the esteemed James Beard Rising Star Award. Just three years later, Daniela was the youngest chef to be named World's Best Female Chef by the renowned list The World's Best 50 Restaurants. It was an incredible honor for a chef who hadn't quite reached age thirty! More accolades, honors, and awards followed.

But Daniela isn't focused on recognition or fame. Her goal remains to combine traditional recipes with local ingredients and create something old—and new. She excels at blending different cultures and cooking styles together. And always with joy and happiness.

And one day, she hopes to open a cooking school for children to pass down her knowledge and enthusiasm to a new generation of budding chefs.

FIRST AID KIT

MARY SEACOLE

* HEROIC HEALER *

As a child growing up in Jamaica, Mary carefully watched her mother gather herbs to make medicines. She also accompanied her on visits to the sick. When Mary wasn't helping her mother, she practiced her doctoring skills by bandaging animals and tending to her dolls. By twelve years old, she was caring for the sick on her own!

Mary's other passion was traveling—she sailed all over the Caribbean and Central America, picking up more medical knowledge wherever she went.

During her youth, two deadly epidemics broke out—yellow fever and cholera. Without hesitation, Mary rushed in to tend the sick and dying, despite the risk to her own health.

In 1853, when the Crimean War broke out, Mary sailed to London, marched into the British War Office, and volunteered her services as a nurse.

She was turned down because she lacked professional training, relied on herbal remedies, and was almost fifty years old and biracial.

But that didn't stop Mary.

She paid her own way to Crimea and again volunteered to help.

And again, was turned down.

So, Mary simply built a makeshift hospital with driftwood, broken wooden crates, and salvaged materials. She called it the British Hotel, and it was soon filled with recovering soldiers. Mary cooked healthy meals and tended to their wounds. When soldiers were too injured to come to her, she went directly onto the battlefield to render aid. Mary dodged bullets and bombs to care for soldiers—no matter what side they fought on. Her gentle manner earned her the nickname "Mother Seacole," and although she never had children of her own, she viewed all her patients as family.

Finally, in February 1856, the war ended. Mary was exhausted. And broke. She'd spent every cent she earned to buy bandages and food for recovering soldiers.

But a journalist—one of the very first to report from the front lines—had written about Mary's exploits for the *London Times*. When she returned to London, friends, supporters, and even Queen Victoria raised money for her to publish her autobiography, *Wonderful Adventures of Mrs. Seacole in Many Lands*.

Mary has many buildings named after her in both England and Jamaica, and she has inspired generations of caregivers to follow in her footsteps and selflessly care for those in need.

ANNIE DODGE WAUNEKA

ACCOMPLISHED ACTIVIST

Annie's father was an important Navajo leader, and she spent her early years helping care for the family's animals. By the age of five, she was skilled at herding her own small flock of sheep.

While attending boarding school at eight years old, the Spanish influenza pandemic struck. The school was quarantined with only one nurse to care for over two hundred children. Annie recovered quickly and spent her time caring for the other ill students. This experience would foster a lifelong interest in healthcare issues.

As a young woman, Annie married and endured years of problematic pregnancies because of the lack of medical care on the Navajo reservation. She was determined to do something about it.

Annie became involved in Navajo tribal politics and traveled with her father, translating for him during meetings. In 1951, she won a position on the Navajo Tribal Council—now when she advocated for better health care, more hospitals on the reservation, and routine vaccines, people listened.

Another deadly disease called tuberculosis became rampant and many people refused to leave the reservation to seek treatment. Annie educated herself about the disease and became chair of the newly designed health and welfare committee—a position she held for the next twenty-seven years. She began visiting hospitals and homes to educate the public on tuberculosis—and other healthcare issues.

Annie didn't stop there. The language barrier was a problem in getting proper information to patients, so she translated an English medical dictionary into Navajo. She also created educational films on health care and aired a weekly radio broadcast.

Many people didn't want to be hospitalized away from their family. Without phones, they couldn't communicate with each other. Annie stepped in to help. She would record messages on a tape recorder and drive back and forth from the hospital to her patient's home, relaying their messages. It was time-consuming and tedious. But to Annie, it was worth it.

Annie also made frequent trips to Washington, DC, where she spoke to government officials and Congress. She advocated for better education, clean water, affordable housing, and women's health issues—especially mother and child care.

Among other awards, Annie was the first Native American woman to receive the Presidential Medal of Freedom in 1963, and in 1976, she was selected as *Ladies' Home Journal*'s Woman of the Year for devoting her life to improving the lives of others.

BIBLIOGRAPHY

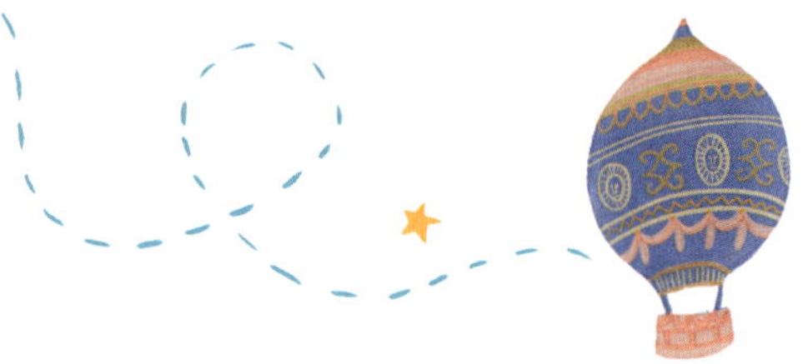

Adams, Julia. *101 Awesome Women Who Changed the World*. London: Arcturus, 2019.

Adams, Tom. *KidStory—50 Children and Young People Who Shook Up the World*. New York: Atheneum Books for Young Readers, 2020.

Alexander, Rae. "The Chinese-American Doctor Who Raised Hell—and 1,500 WWII Servicemen." *KQED* podcast, August 27, 2021.

Alibhai-Brown, Yasmin. *Ladies Who Punch*. London: Biteback Publishing Ltd., 2020.

Atkins, Jeannine. *Girls Who Looked Under Rocks—The Lives of Six Pioneering Naturalists*. Nevada City: Dawn Publications, 2000.

Becker, Elizabeth. *You Don't Belong Here*. New York: Public Affairs, 2021.

Beckmann, Anne-Marie. *Women War Photographers—From Lee Miller to Anja Niedringhaus*. New York: Prestel, 2019.

Billioud, Jean-Michel. *Amazing Athletes—40 Inspiring Icons*. Minneapolis: Quarto Publishing, 2020.

Boxer, Elisa. *SPLASH! Ethelda Bleibtrey Makes Waves of Change*. Ann Arbor: Sleeping Bear Press, 2022.

Buckley, James, Jr. *Fight for Life! Rain Forest Survivor*. Minneapolis: Bearport Publishing, 2023.

Cavallo, Francesca, and Elena Favilli. *Good Night Stories for Rebel Girls 2*. Canada: Timbuktu Labs, 2017.

Cho, Tina. *Asian American Women in Science—15 Inspiring People You Should Know*. Oakland: Rockridge Press, 2022.

Clarke, Gemma. *Soccerwomen—The Icons, Rebels, Stars, and Trailblazers Who Transformed The Beautiful Game*. New York: Bold Type Books, 2019.

Clinton, Hillary Rodham, and Chelsea Clinton. *The Book of Gutsy Women*. New York: Simon & Schuster, 2019.

Copperfield, David, Richard Wiseman, and David Britland. *David Copperfield's History of Magic*. New York: Simon & Schuster, 2021.

Dagg, Anne Innis. *5 Giraffes*. Markham: Fitzhenry & Whiteside, 2016.

Daluge, Agnes Lackovic, and Willard Daluge. *Rosa's Miracle Mouse—The True Story of a WWII Undercover Teenager*. Hopkins: Author's Direct Books, 1998.

Davidson, Robyn. *TRACKS—A Woman's Solo Trek Across 1,700 Miles of Australian Outback*. New York: Vintage Departures Editions, 1980.

DePrince, Michaela. *Taking Flight—From War Orphan to Star Ballerina*. New York: Alfred Knopf, 2014.

Diana, Julie. "The Next Chapter." *Dance Spirit* 19, no. 7 (September 2015): 68–74.

Farrell, Mary Cronk. *Close-Up on War: The Story of Pioneering Photojournalist Catherine Leroy in Vietnam*. New York: Amulet Books, 2022.

Favilli, Elena. *Good Night Stories for Rebel Girls—100 Immigrant Women Who Changed the World*. Canada: Timbuktu Labs, Inc., 2020.

Gibson, Karen Bush. *Women Aviators: 26 Stories of Pioneer Flights, Daring Missions, and Record-Setting Journeys*. Chicago: Chicago Review Press, 2013.

"Girl Dare-Devil to Thrill Air Fans." *The San Bernadino County Sun*, October 7, 1928.

Godin, Melissa. "Australian Explorer Robyn Davidson on the Value of Solitude in the Pandemic Era." *Time Magazine*, July 16, 2020.

Griffith, Evan. *Secrets of the Sea—The Story of Jeanne Power, Revolutionary Marine Scientist*. New York: Clarion Books, 2021.

Hearst, Michael. *Extraordinary People*. San Francisco: Chronicle Books, 2015.

Henderson, Leah. *Mamie on the Mound—A Woman in Baseball's Negro Leagues*. North Mankato: Capstone, 2020.

Hill, Julia Butterfly. *The Legacy of Luna—The Story of a Tree, a Woman, and the Struggle to Save the Redwoods*. New York: HarperCollins Publishers, 2000.

"Interview with Daniela Soto-Innes." *Hospitality Design* 38, no. 8 (October 2016): 107–17.

Isaacs, Sally. *Helen Thayer's Arctic Adventure: A Woman and a Dog Walk to the North Pole*. North Mankato: Capstone Young Readers, 2016.

Johnson, Robin C. *FEARLESS—Gutsy Gals of a Bygone Era*. Monee: California Venture Books, 2017.

Johnston, Julia De Laurentiis. *Her Epic Adventure—25 Daring Women Who Inspire a Life Less Ordinary*. Toronto: Kids Can Press, 2021.

Keating, Jess. *The Girl Who Built an Ocean—An Artist, An Argonaut, and the True Story of the World's First Aquarium*. New York: Alfred A. Knopf, 2022.

Kuhne, Cecil, ed. *Near Death in the Desert—True Stories of Disaster and Survival*. New York: Vintage Departures, 2009.

Kyi, Tanya Lloyd. *When the Worst Happens—Extraordinary Stories of Survival*. New York: Annick Press, 2014.

Lang, Heather. *The Leaf Detective—How Margaret Lowman Uncovered Secrets in the Rainforest*. New York: Calkins Creek, 2021.

Lawrence, Sandra. *Anthology of Amazing Women—Trailblazers Who Dared to be Different*. New York: Little Bee Books, 2017.

Lee, Mackenzi. *Bygone Badass Broads—52 Forgotten Women Who Changed the World*. New York: Abrams, 2018.

Letts, Elizabeth. *The Ride of Her Life—The True Story of a Woman, Her Horse, and Their Last-Chance Journey Across America*. New York: Ballantine Books, 2021.

Lowe, Mifflin. *The True West: Real Stories About Black Cowboys, Women Sharpshooters, Native American Rodeo Stars, Pioneering Vaqueros, and the Unsung Explorers, Builders, and Heroes Who Shaped the American West*. Fresno: Bushel & Peck Books, 2020.

Machajewski, David. *Marta*. New York: PowerKids Press, 2019.

McCullough, Joy. *Harriet's Ruffled Feathers—The Woman Who Saved Millions of Birds*. New York: Atheneum Books for Young Readers, 2022.

Miles, Rosalind. *The Women's History of the Modern World*. New York: William Morrow, 2021.

Miller, Kenneth, and Alan Sheldon. "Saving the Last Orangutans." *Life* 21, no, 6 (May 1998): 66.

Mitchell, John H. "The Mothers of Conservation." *Sanctuary: The Journal of the Massachusetts Audubon Society*, February 1996, 1–20.

Montgomery, Sy. *Walking with the Great Apes—Jane Goodall, Dian Fossey, Biruté Galdikas*. White River Junction: Chelsea Green Publishing, 2009.

Mrazek, Robert J. *The Indomitable Florence Finch—The Untold Story of a War Widow Turned Resistance Fighter and Savior of American POWs*. New York: Hachette Books, 2020.

Nienow, Tootie. *There Goes Patti McGee!* New York: Farrar Strauss Giroux, 2021.

Niethammer, Carolyn. *I'll Go and Do More: Annie Dodge Wauneka, Navajo Leader and Activist*. Lincoln: University of Nebraska Press, 2007.

Nyad, Diana. *Find a Way*. New York: Alfred A. Knopf, 2015.

O'Brien, Kerrie. "Wild at Heart: Robyn Davidson, 40 Years on from Tracks." *The Sydney Morning Herald*, October 31, 2020.

Olsen, Steve. "Patti McGee Interview." *Juice Magazine*, July 20, 2017.

Piastro, Dianne B. "How the Disabled Won Independence." *Del Rio News Herald*, August 16, 1990.

Pimentel, Annette Bay. *All the Way to the Top—How One Girl's Fight for Americans with Disabilities Changed Everything*. Naperville: Sourcebooks, 2020.

Ponvannan, Gayathri. *Unstoppable: 75 Stories of Trailblazing Indian Women*. India: Hachette, 2019.

"Protestors dramatize rights of disabled." *The Kerryville Times*, March 13, 1990.

Rainsford, Blair. "From Survivor to Star." *Scholastic Action* 36, no. 5 (November 2012): 10–13.

Reed, Darcy. *Extraordinary Women with Cameras—35 Photographers Who Changed How We See the World*. San Rafael: Rocky Nook, 2022.

Reynolds, Graham, with Wanda Robson. *Viola Desmond: Her Life and Times*. Nova Scotia: Roseway Publishing, 2018.

Robbins, Dean. *The Fastest Girl on Earth!* New York: Alfred A. Knopf, 2021.

Robinson, Fiona. *The Bluest of Blues—Anna Atkins and the First Book of Photographs*. New York: Abrams Books for Young Readers, 2019.

Rockliff, Mara. *Anything but Ordinary Addie—The True Story of Adelaide Herrmann, Queen of Magic*. Somerville: Candlewick Press, 2016.

Ross, Alisa. *The Girl Who Rode a Shark & Other Stories of Daring Women*. Toronto: Pajama Press, 2019.

Ross, Michael Elsohn. *A World of Her Own—24 Amazing Women Explorers and Adventurers*. Chicago: Chicago Review Press, 2014.

Rothman, Lily. "A 14-Year-Old Girl Sailed Around the World—and She Brought a Camera." *Time.com*, January 21, 2013.

Rubin, Susan Goldman. *Mary Seacole: Bound for the Battlefield*. Somerville: Candlewick Press, 2020.

Sarkeesian, Anita, and Ebony Adams. *History vs Women—The Defiant Lives That They Don't Want You to Know*. New York: Feiwel and Friends, 2018.

Schatz, Kate. *Rad Women Worldwide—Artists and Athletes, Pirates and Punks, and Other Revolutionaries Who Shaped History*. Berkeley: Ten Speed Press, 2016.

Shen, Ann. *Bad Girls Throughout History—100 Remarkable Women Who Changed the World*. San Francisco: Chronicle Books, 2016.

Shindler, Karolyn. *Discovering Dorothea—The Life of the Pioneering Fossil-Hunter Dorothea Bate*. London: HarperCollins, 2005.

Singer, Toba. "Remembering Alicia Alonso, Cuba's Prima Ballerina." *Pointe*, October 16, 2019.

Staaf, Danna. *The Lady and the Octopus: How Jeanne Villepreux-Power Invented Aquariums And Revolutionized Marine Biology*. Minneapolis: Carolrhoda Books, 2022.

Stanford, Jill Charlotte. *Wild Women & Tricky Ladies—Rodeo Cowgirls, Trick Riders, and Other Performing Women Who Made the West Wilder*. Guilford: TwoDot, 2011.

Swaby, Rachel. *Trailblazers: 33 Women in Science Who Changed the World*. New York: Delacorte Press, 2016.

Thacher, Alida. *Fastest Woman on Earth*. Milwaukee: Raintree Publishers, 1980.

Thayer, Helen. "Climb Your Mountain." *Highlights for Children* 61, no. 4 (April 2006): 27.

Thayer, Helen. *Walking the Gobi*. Seattle: The Mountaineers Books, 2007.

Viña, Rose. *Alicia Alonso Dances On*. Chicago: Albert Whitman & Company, 2021.

Warner, Jody Nyasha, and Richard Rudnicki. *Viola Desmond Won't be Budged!* Toronto: Groundwood Books, 2010.

Wigo, Bruce. "Did You Know About Ethelda Bleibtrey?" *Swimming World* 62, no. 8 (August 2021): 9.

Willson, Margaret. *Woman, Captain, Rebel—The Extraordinary True Story of a Daring Icelandic Sea Captain*. Naperville: Sourcebooks, 2023.

Wilson, Jamia. *Young, Gifted, and Black*. Beverly: Wide Eyed Editions, 2018.

Wolf, Analiza Quiroz. *Asian-Americans Who Inspire Us*. Wishful Wolf Press, 2019.

Wright, Sharon. *Balloonomania Belles—Daredevil Divas Who First Took to the Sky*. South Yorkshire: Pen & Sword History, 2018.

INDEX OF THE WOMEN WHO DARED

© Read Photography

ABOUT THE AUTHOR

Linda Skeers loves searching for amazing people and fascinating tidbits in history for her nonfiction projects and writing a line that makes her snort out loud for her fiction projects. She's co-taught the Whispering Woods Picture Book Writing Workshop for more than twenty years and loves to mentor other writers on their publishing journey. She lives in Iowa.

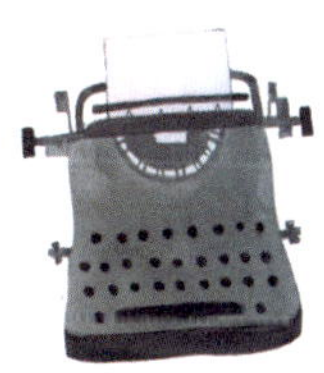

© Livi Gosling

ABOUT THE ILLUSTRATOR

Livi Gosling is an illustrator from the UK. She studied in Cornwall and now lives in Hertfordshire. When she's not drawing, she can be found tending to her vegetable patch or reading books with her young daughter. Visit her at livigosling.co.uk.